"People think the hard thing about business leadership is coming up with the next breakthrough idea. What is truly hard is bringing the idea to life in such a way that it is not only embraced but celebrated by employees, partners, and customers. Kelly Keenan brings his client-tested branding method to life in this fluff-free, eminently practical, and totally inspirational book and proves that 'authentic influencer' is not an oxymoron."

—**PAMELA SLIM**, award-winning & best-selling author,
Body of Work and *The Widest Net*

"Simply put, Kelly Keenan gets what it means to truly craft a brand story the right way. The system and framework he's created are applicable for any business, regardless of size or type. If you're finally ready to get your company's brand story where it needs to be, I highly recommend EIAI."

—**MARCUS SHERIDAN**, international keynote speaker on digital sales/marketing, ranked #1 LinkedIn Voices for Entrepreneurship, and author of *They Ask, You Answer*

"Influence is an outcome, not a job description. Keenan masterfully re-frames how to think about influence, moving it from a transactional social media play to a bigger picture way of thinking about business. Having written a book on influencer marketing out of the frustrations surrounding the misconceptions of influence, I tend to be highly cynical, but this book nails it. Keenan understands how crucial influencer connection is, that it's not just about views, likes, but about values, mutual goals, and synchrony, and provides a road map to long-term culture, relationship, and sales success."

—**AMANDA RUSSELL**, author, *The Influencer Code*,
speaker, and marketing strategist

"What if you could become a change-maker and influencer in your organization, industry, and relationships? Now you can! Kelly Keenan has been one of the world's top experts in brand and culture over the last 20 years, and now he shares his proven process in this trail-blazing book. This important work is not only thought-provoking ... it is CHANGE-provoking. Start reading it today and watch your transformation."

—**ED TSENG**, TEDx speaker, Olympic coach, Pro of the Year, and best-selling author, *Game. Set. Life. Peak Performance for Sports and Life*

"Influence is synonymous with leadership. If you are truly an influencer, you are a leader. This book is a strategic road map for you and/or your organization to create a culture and pathway for true change and impact. Digest this work as you would a transformational plan. You will be better for having taken the time to read and apply every truth."

—**MIKE STAVER**, author, *Leadership Isn't for Cowards*, speaker, and architect of *Training* magazine's 2018 #1 Training Program in the World

—

Everyone
is an
"Influencer"

—

KELLY KEENAN

—

Everyone
is an
"Influencer"

—

BUILDING A BRAND BY ENGAGING THE
PEOPLE WHO MATTER MOST

IDEAPRESS
PUBLISHING

WASHINGTON, D.C.

IDEAPRESS
PUBLISHING

Copyright © 2021 by Kelly Keenan

Printed in the United States.

Ideapress Publishing | www.ideapresspublishing.com

Cover Design: Jeff Miller, Faceout Studios
Interior Design: Jessica Angerstein

Cataloging-in-Publication Data is on file with the Library of Congress.

ISBN: 978-1-64687-011-0

Special Sales
Ideapress Books are available at a special discount for bulk purchases for sales promotions and premiums, or for use in corporate training programs. Special editions, including personalized covers, a custom foreword, corporate imprints, and bonus content, are also available.

This book is dedicated to the Brand Story Experts who have been committed to executing and advancing our process since 2009. Thank you for joining me on this journey. Your support and enthusiasm inspire me and truly make the work we do feel like a celebration.

CONTENTS

How to Engage the People Who Really Matter (And Ignore Those Who Don't)

BRAND STORIES ARE my life's work. The simple concept that a company's story can bring out its best is an idea I adopted early in my career. It changed the way I work with clients and captivated me from the start. Few things are more inspiring than helping an organization clarify with pride what strengthens its culture and improves the experience for everyone. In 2009, I closed my agency of ten years to focus on that one thing: telling, refining, and celebrating stories, and using those stories to engage influencers of all levels.

I have been blessed to work with hundreds of companies across industries as diverse as home services, construction and technology, and even the Pittsburgh Pirates, to discover stories that inspire internal and external influencers. However, as the central theme of this book will verify, your brand experience and culture get better when you share the experience with like-minded individuals. Today I work with a team of brand story experts, refining a process that I am excited to share with you.

You will learn about the following topics:

- The opportunity to celebrate your story
- The process of Culture Development Marketing (CDM)
- What brands are (and what they are not)
- Who is an influencer (and who is not)
- How to create a story-driven culture full of energy, appreciation, and success
- Why the single biggest opportunity in business today is realizing that everyone is an influencer

If you are reading these bullet points and questioning whether this is a book for you, a quick way to end the indecision is to simply ask yourself, "Am I interested in learning how to bring more happiness, stability, and success to my company?" If this interests you, then yes, this book is for you.

No, really!

Judging from the title, you may feel that the quickest way to do all of that is by adding **influencers**. But influencers are not the solution—they are the result. The goal is to build trusted relationships by establishing a culture that celebrates shared vision and values. Once you do that, you are winning.

This book will explain why the truest influence is earned through interaction, involvement, and participation. This game-changing perspective can be used personally and professionally to become a stronger leader, team member, parent, or coach.

Perhaps you feel that the terms **brand story** and **influencer** have become so overused that it is difficult to imagine a fresh story development process in the world of business. You will find that although I conceived and trademarked my story development process in 2009, the main mechanisms and principles are still ahead of the game today.

THIS PROCESS WORKS FOR EVERY COMPANY THAT'S ALL IN.

Our agency has specialized in brand stories from the start, and the need for what we do continues to grow. In fact, in the past two years, our agency has experienced more than 200 percent revenue growth and tripled the size of our team ... while dealing with global uncertainty and a pandemic.

We are building brand clarity, helping leaders gain strength, and creating company celebrations that supercharge brand experiences. We bring out the best in every brand by shining a light on their most inspiring aspects. However, for the process to work, the organization must be committed, stay on board, and go all in. Our brand story experts are passionate about helping brands who are inspired to build their company, solidify their culture, and celebrate their stories.

This book will explain the concepts that drive my success and the success of my clients, and how these breakthroughs will transform your business and culture. Profiles of companies and leaders with a gift for understanding influence and influencers are shared. You'll understand the unique power of celebrating your brand story and how your celebration is amplified through the passionate participation of true influencers. You'll learn why these are the people who really matter and why you should be ignoring those who don't. This book will help you gain clarity, empower your organization, and set your brand on a path to continual growth and success.

CHAPTER ONE

The Story Sharing Shift

I N 1973, THE public chatter was about Hall of Fame quarterback Joe Namath's legs. As a spokesmodel for Hanes, he participated in a now-(in)famous campaign where he wore pantyhose. The campaign made a huge impact because Namath was the biggest name in sports at the time. He was an "Influencer."

That 50-year-old campaign illustrates that influencers associating with brands is not a new idea. However, the definition of **influencer** has evolved far beyond the idea of athletes and celebrities endorsing brands. Hiring influencers has grown into an opportunity that impacts and involves every area of business.

Organizations in this era needs to acknowledge, understand, and pursue influencers. The need for such individuals has largely come about because workforce mentality has shifted. Business ideas and innovation now happen beyond management meetings in the board-room. Team members fill every type of position, and supporters outside the brand can dramatically influence the images and outcomes associated with companies.

—

YES, THERE IS NO "I" IN TEAM,
BUT THERE IS AN "I" IN INFLUENCER.

—

The opportunity to step up and be an influencer, to impact a brand's story and create change, is open to everyone. This transformational shift has made a brand story strategy mandatory for leaders at all levels. From the CEO to the Marketing Department to a new team member looking to make a difference, this book is for you.

GETTING IT WRONG WILL TANK YOUR BUSINESS

Most businesses are already looking for ways to take advantage of the opportunity to utilize influencers. Some companies are making huge gains, creating demand, and absolutely crushing it with influencer partnerships, and others want in. Influencer marketing seems like a no-brainer. But what can happen if you get it wrong?

Before you rush in, remember that the story has to be right and the influencer relationship has to be believable—more than a feigned celebrity endorsement. Only a real, authentic relationship will build credibility and trust, and influence your brand.

Tiger Woods and Shaq endorsed Oldsmobile and Buick. Did anyone ever believe that they would choose those cars if they weren't paid millions to endorse them?

Association makes an impact. It can build trust or ruin credibility, and the stakes have been raised significantly in the 21st century. The opportunity for success is surely present, but a negative blow from a disengaged influencer can destroy a business.

Brands take a risk whenever they work with someone. Celebrities with clean images can fall from grace quickly, and any celebrity can have their integrity attacked. If a company has to withdraw support for a public figure after they did or said something considered objectionable or offensive, the brand will suffer.

The number of social media influencers is skyrocketing, but the credibility of this advertising model is diminishing at the same speed. Gone are the days where any celebrity could be hired to say nice things about you and your company while you let the money roll in.

Sure, the opportunities are bigger than ever. But unfortunately, there are also more implementation questions than ever. Get your campaign wrong and the move could tank your business. However, if you get it right, it won't matter if your brand loses a key influencer. You'll have the tools to pivot and adapt.

—

KNOW THE STAKES SO YOU CAN CHOOSE YOUR INFLUENCER ASSOCIATIONS WISELY.

—

NOT JUST CELEBRITIES

Celebrity endorsement won't guarantee gains for your company. Celebrities can amplify a company's message and expand their audience, but if the company and the celebrity's interests are at odds, it could hurt the reputation of both parties.

- The company could have an influx of customers they can't help.
- The celebrity's endorsement could hurt future deals due to a lack of credibility.
- Customers could be let down by not getting a good product.

Sharing your story the right way—focusing on the true aspects of your brand—will help you gain the right influencer relationships. It will also help you become a better leader, get more out of your job, and be a part of something far more meaningful. Learning to celebrate your brand story in this manner builds and strengthens internal and external relationships.

LET'S GET REAL ABOUT INFLUENCERS

Putting your trust in someone to gain insight, borrow their perspective, or learn from their evaluation is a long-standing, effective strategy. People have always had the ability to influence and inspire others in this way.

However, in the past decade, this idea has expanded as the concept of **influencer marketing** has exploded. Social media has equipped people with these global platforms to create widespread presentations of their personality, ideas, and opinions. The emergence of social channels has not only amplified the voice of the individual; it has also provided the opportunity to form a data-defined definition labeling their impact.

As a result, the term **influencer** has become a quantifiable marketing definition. Professionals now identify tiers of Instagram influencers, from mega-influencer, macro-influencer, mid-tier-influencer, micro-influencer, all the way down to a nano-influencer.

You can also label expert subgroups in categories like Celebrity, Lifestyle Blogger, Traveler, Beauty Blogger, Product Blogger, Fashion Stylist, Vlogger, Photographer, Thought Leader, and more. The term **influencer** has been outlined, examined, and defined in nearly every way you can imagine.

So, is it settled? Do we finally have a final definition of who an influencer is and what they are all about?

Not even close.

Brand experts are certainly trying. These tiered classifications and subcategories are valuable tools to help identify a person's ability to create sales and drive interest through their influence. But they are merely a useful starting point.

There are too many variables to measure an influencer's true ability to partner with a brand. Wishful brands often overestimate the impact of an influencer and are left with disappointed stakeholders, wasted money, and weak sales. In addition, too many brands overlook the power of smaller, more passionate influencers. It's important to realize that you can't count anyone out as an influencer. Whether someone is or isn't an influencer depends on the brand that is asking and the context of the relationship.

INDUSTRY INFLUENCERS ARE HIDING IN PLAIN SIGHT

Pat Cleary probably won't make the Nike, Budweiser, or Verizon list of prime influencers, but at the ClientSpace User Conference, nobody was more valuable. Mr. Cleary is the President of NAPEO, a critical organization for anyone in the professional employer organization (PEO) industry. My client, NetWise Technology, was in that game.

NetWise Technology was a smaller company in the PEO industry, but they had a tremendous product called ClientSpace. The NetWise team believed in the quality of their product and the solutions it designed—they just needed help coordinating and celebrating their story. We did just that. The new brand shift was followed by tremendous growth, record sales years, and so much success that they became attractive enough to be acquired.

One of the new NetWise initiatives we helped launch was an annual ClientSpace User Conference. The event showcased their product, team, and culture. It also provided an opportunity for the NetWise team to bring in industry influencers to celebrate their company, product solutions, and culture. Every year, as their company's sales grew, the conference attendance grew.

However, instead of looking to upgrade their featured speaker each year, NetWise President Randy Wadle remained emphatic that his "main goal every year was to secure the participation of NAPEO President Pat Cleary." Randy was certain that he was NetWise's biggest influencer. Randy stated that "Pat gets what we do and brings value to this event that nobody else can deliver." In this arena, Pat Cleary was the influencer who mattered most.

—

IT'S ALL ABOUT REAL AUTHENTICITY, NOT JUST BIG NUMBERS.

—

Influencer integration is vital to determining their impact. For this reason, it is impossible to definitively classify anyone as an authentic influencer at any level. First it has to be determined if the individual has the desire and ability to become integrated and involved with the brand. An influencer only matters and makes sense for the brand if they possess the ability to be attached to or engaged with the brand's story in a real and relatable way.

This attachment isn't based on the size of the audience they reach, or the level of celebrity status they bring with them. Everyone can be an influencer, and the impact they make multiplies when they're brought together with other like-minded influencers who celebrate the same story:

- A single salesperson who steps up and consistently celebrates success stories makes a profound impact by continuously reinforcing their company's reputation for service excellence. Not only are they powerful influencers, but their participation can be a force that saves or strengthens the company.

- An emotional customer who joins a social media platform to post their first video ever explaining how a nutrition company changed their life can go viral and inspire millions of people. This type of internet hype is unpredictable because the right story, at the right time, can happen at any time.

These are just two of the many variables that make it challenging to measure influencer impact accurately or define it definitively. As hard as people try to explain the term, title, and power of an influencer, single definitions are tough to gauge.

—

POWERFUL PERSONAL INFLUENCE
CAN COME FROM ANYWHERE.

—

A mega-influencer can be a college professor who's never even been on social media but once took the time to tell you an inspiring story that caused you to stick it out in your major. Her influence gave you the courage to chase your dreams.

Another game-changing influencer can be a team member who rarely speaks up. Still, he has spent a decade arriving at work an hour early, contributing passionately, and is always willing to help others in any way.

These insiders may not have a platform they use to map out ways for them to gain attention, add followers, or build an audience, but they create a rare influence that inspires others around them to do more and be more.

In our world, talk about the power of influence is everywhere. While the idea is popular, overuse of the technique is causing many to miss out on the benefits that authentic influence offers. Don't lose sight of the fact that authentic influence is a product of participation and integration. That is what matters most, and those are the people who matter most.

DON'T TAKE SHORTCUTS WHEN DETERMINING WHO INFLUENCERS ARE

Many view Influencer Marketing as a cheat code. They seek out partnerships with celebrities to buy their way into benefitting from the influencer's authority, knowledge, and social following. These firms don't understand the importance of confirming that their brand's values, beliefs, personality, and interests are aligned with the influencer. Creating real influence isn't about partnering with any celebrity or local boldface name just to produce a relationship with their followers. The best influencer relationships are built on integration, alignment, and shared values. It's a collaboration designed to expand your ability to enlighten and educate customers. Getting people to join the party is what real influence is all about.

Many misunderstand this because they look at influence marketing as a hot, new way to instantly change their brand's image and appeal solely by partnering with personalities. They fail to see the importance of education over influence. They view influencers as marketing tools, and to them, influence is an easy way to generate quick sales. So, they put off learning the best way to share their story. They shortcut the process and fail to create an influencer relationship that educates people on who they are and why they can be trusted.

It's a waste of time.

Now the good news.

Influencer opportunities have expanded far beyond celebrities and social media personalities. *Today, everyone has the potential to be a valuable influencer.*

Any person or community that possesses the credibility and ability to share your brand's story in a way that inspires others to connect, and engages with the story as well, is an influencer. This definition of **influencer** reaches beyond paid influencers to include every individual, regardless of social following or influencer rating. We all have a voice. We also have open access to the internet, social media channels, and email, which provide the ability to communicate our opinions, ideas, and thoughts as frequently as we like in whatever format we choose.

Communities are included in the definition for a reason. People who share a passion or vision can be grouped together to quickly supersize your influencer opportunity. In community influencer relationships, a brand extends their credibility through an association with a group. Such partnerships have existed in the past; however, smart brands have learned to make these relationships

> Any person or community that possesses the credibility and ability to share your brand's story in a way that inspires others to connect, and engages with the story as well, is an influencer.

more meaningful. Their arrangements go far beyond simple alignments and sponsorships to create brand-defining collaborations that can immediately alter a company's trajectory.

At the heart of these expanded influencer opportunities are integration and authenticity.

When people in agreement become integrated with your brand, and they participate with passion, they gain—and give you—authority. But the connection has to be real. The authenticity in their actions allows them to stand out and be recognized.

When a true connection exists, the public learns from what they say, begins to value their own opinions, and becomes inspired to act. Whether that action is purchasing a product, signing up for an email list, or sharing a post on social media, the rare ability to celebrate a brand's story in a way that inspires others to get involved is a truly powerful influence. This impact bubbles up from the experiences, feelings, and dreams of actual people.

Yes, make no mistake about it: The biggest advantage in the world of marketing is the ability to educate the public about your brand's story.

This doesn't mean producing classroom-style lectures on Facebook Live. Organizations need to make education engaging by celebrating brand story-related content, helping people understand the experience. The key is to create a constant flow of content that solves problems, answers questions, introduces new ideas, provides information on products, and makes it easy for people to be a part of what is going on.

—

IF YOUR COMPANY IS IN CRISIS,
CELEBRATING CAN BRING YOU BACK FROM THE DEAD.

—

In 2012, the Best Buy brand story wasn't something they wanted to celebrate. Their CEO had just resigned after admitting to an improper relationship with a female employee, personnel morale had seemingly hit rock bottom, and it appeared they had no plans to compete with Amazon.

A shift needed to happen. New leadership decided to take action by celebrating their story from within. They knew that they needed to inspire their internal influencers first; otherwise, the company was doomed. Employee appreciation and participation became a top priority, and they took intentional steps to show team members that they were valued and supported. A treasured employee discount program was reinstated, they invested heavily in training, and they made it clear that team participation was critical to the company's success.

They began to make changes that were centered on their strengths. They expanded the concept of their popular Geek Squad program to showcase their knowledge and expertise through an In-Home Advisor Program. The service provides in-home visits from Best Buy team members who would act as consultants to offer education and advice.

Next they began using videos of "Blue Shirt" team members to educate customers on new products and tech news. They unleashed these powerful Blue Shirt influencers by giving them a lead role in an ongoing series of insightful videos on Facebook, YouTube, and Instagram. The videos quickly became an important customer resource and a source of pride for the team. It was clear that Best Buy was uniformly celebrating their knowledge, expertise, and employees. This brand story celebration increased customer knowledge and boosted employee morale, while also building the Best Buy culture and brand. The impact was undeniable.

Best Buy operates in a competitive and challenging retail environment, but their focus on education has helped them navigate the waters in expert fashion. In fact, their shift to a brand story celebration has been so transformational that their stock surged from $13 a share in 2012 to over $100 in July 2020. They recognized the opportunity to influence and inspire through brand story development. They embraced it and, ladies and gentleman, Best Buy is back.

—

ALL BUSINESSES (EVEN "BORING" ONES) HAVE THIS OPPORTUNITY.

—

Every business has this same opportunity. Communications tools provide the ability to educate our teams, our customers, and our communities about who we are and what we are all about. However, many brands don't link the Influencer opportunity to education. Instead, they believe that they don't need to spend time educating because paid influencers can get people to purchase nearly anything. These brands have no problem finding influencer partners who will sell and say anything for money. Credibility is crumbling, and the issue is only intensifying.

A QUICK WORD ABOUT THE FTC

According to a Mediakix study, paid influencer marketing has grown to a $10 billion industry, and as the number of paid influencers grows, so do the trust issues surrounding their recommendations. In 2017, the Federal Trade Commission (FTC) began filing cases against individual influencers after discovering that 93 percent of top celebrities on Instagram do not follow FTC guidelines on proper brand sponsorship disclosure. Influencers are now required to highlight paid partnerships clearly. With so many influencers, it is difficult to police them all, and many influencers and brands have failed to take the FTC guidelines seriously. That may be changing, as the FTC has moved on from simply issuing warnings.

In 2018, the agency issued a formal admonition to detox tea company Teami. The FTC warning clearly advised the Florida-based tea company that all connections between endorsers and advertisers must be disclosed and viewable. Teami, like many other brands, refused to take the warning seriously. In 2020, Teami was charged with making false claims about the benefits of their teas. They were also breaking guideline rules: Burying sponsored post descriptions on Instagram from well-known entertainers and influencers who were endorsing these fallacies.

The FTC bluntly indicated that they had seen enough of Teami's deceptive practices and handed down a $15 million judgment. However, based on the company's financial condition, the $15 million fine was partially suspended upon the payment of $1 million.

The FTC thus made a strong statement, but the struggle continues. Fake influencer issues are not difficult to find as many brands and influencers continue to play deceptive games. It remains to be seen if these issues can be effectively halted. Influence shouldn't be about whether you get caught or not.

Companies can avoid getting engaged in the hype by remembering that real influencer associations are about collaborating to build relationships through trust. To honor these bonds, brands need to be certain that the influencer relationship is authentic. The public gets upset when they witness influencer relationships that don't feel real and relevant.

—

CAUTION: NO INFLUENCER CAN SAVE YOU FROM A BAD STORY.

—

Pepsi learned this lesson firsthand in April 2017, when they posted an ad on YouTube starring Kendall Jenner. The 2.5-minute video showed a marching group of people holding "Join the Conversation" signs that also made nonspecific references to police brutality and Black Lives Matter protests. The protestors are smiling, laughing, and appear to be having the time of their lives. The weird music video builds to a "climactic" scene where Kendall Jenner grabs a can of Pepsi, steps up to a stone-faced police officer monitoring the protest, and hands it to him. The officer smiles, drinks the Pepsi, and the crowd cheers.

The problem was that viewers didn't cheer, and the result was not as inspiring as Pepsi had hoped. The vision of a white, 21-year-old supermodel influencer prancing into a protest to solve the issues of police brutality and racial injustice—simply by sharing a Pepsi—was just too much to take. How bad was the response?

- So bad that Pepsi had to pull the ad in just one day for "missing the mark" with their message. They also apologized for "putting Kendall Jenner in this position."

- So bad that the internet and media outlets exploded with comments, stories, and scathing criticism of the ad.

- So bad that Bernice King, the daughter of Martin Luther King Jr., tweeted a photo that showed her father being restrained by police with the caption, "If only Daddy would have known about the power of #Pepsi."

- So bad that as protests denouncing police violence and the death of George Floyd grew across the world in 2020, screenshots of the 2017 Pepsi ad began resurfacing all over the internet.

This is a tremendous example of the importance of authenticity over popularity. Kendall Jenner is, in fact, one of the most powerful influencers in the world, with over 170 million Instagram followers. Her influence is clearly valuable, as she reportedly makes over $600,000 per sponsored post. However, an influencer's power is only beneficial to a brand if they are aligned and integrated with it in an authentic way.

Paying for influencers who feel no loyalty to you, aren't integrated with your message, and have no investment in your success is a risky marketing approach. This type of shallow partnership can damage your brand, and even turn the public against your company.

If relationships with paid influencers are handled correctly, they can be the most influential component of your brand story celebration. In fact, paid influencers build excitement, interest, and trust in a way that is tough to beat. This type of power will continue to grow as influencers and brands learn to work together to create true partnerships that make sense. The paid influencers who are doing it right make a big impact for brands that have the resources, connections, and budget to partner with them. But right now, too many influencers are not only failing to do it right, but are also doing it for the wrong reasons.

Stories are present all over the internet about bridezilla bloggers attempting to gain gratis wedding photos and video packages, food critics looking for complimentary meals, or travel bloggers seeking free hotels. Oftentimes, the targeted service providers are restaurants, bars, or hotels that buckle under pressure and give influencers what they demand. Conceding is an easier route than dealing with negative publicity, reviews, and backlash. Many businesses are fed up with the bullying.

A great example of how out of hand the strongarming from influencers can be happened in October 2019, when an "influencer" gave a restaurant a one-star Yelp review despite admitting that the restaurant served some of the "best Italian food" they have ever had. The anonymous influencer apparently left the one-star review to teach the restaurant's manager a lesson. The influencer's review boldly announced that she had told the manager how much she enjoyed the food, and mentioned to the server that she planned to post a review celebrating the food to her 11,000 followers on Yelp. However, when she got the check and her influencer status hadn't resulted in a discount or freebie, she blasted the restaurant by giving them one star. Fortunately, a Reddit user saw the ridiculous review and reposted it as an example of how outlandish "influencers" can be.

☆☆☆☆☆ 10/2/2019

I'm giving 1 star because of the cheap management and customer service. I heard the food was very good so I went to try. Me and the BF got the calamari, spaghetti alle vongole, and gnocchi. All were very delicious.

I was actually so impressed that when the manager came to ask us how everything tasted I told her it was some of the best Italian food Ive had and I told her Im going to post about it on Instagram where I have over 11 thousand followers and a lot of them are in the area. She seemed very happy about it.

I was wrong. I thought that she would be greatful for the free advertising but when the check came there was literally no discount at all. I thought at least one of the entrees would be taken off but they didnt even take off the calamari or even the drinks!

I wont go back here because of this. Which is a shame because the food was very good. The manager needs to understand how to treat customers.

Business owners aren't the only folks who have had enough. Consumers are now sounding off against entitled influencers whenever a story of influencer abuse is shared. In addition, brands have gotten wise to the threats, becoming well aware that many influencers are only looking to game their way to free products, perks, and paychecks. The targeted brands are standing up to the pressure. The smoke and mirrors these influencers are using are not the way to build trust: Real relationships are built on authenticity.

Brands need to look beyond the number of followers an influencer has and consider their authenticity before anything else, whether it's an industry business leader who is known for being an innovator or a customer who has a unique take on your story.

THE BEST TOOLS MAY ALREADY BE IN YOUR TOOLBOX

Influencers are everywhere, and some of your most valuable influencers are probably right underneath your nose: your team members and other stakeholders in your firm. These employees have the most to offer in celebrating your brand story because they have the most access, opportunity, and ability to influence consistently. They also have the highest amount of credibility. The ideas and information they share allow the public to peek into their employer relationship.

Best Buy is a big brand with enough marketing dollars to hire any influencer in the world. They could have gained traction by negotiating a big-time paid influencer partnership. That influencer could have served as an ongoing spokesperson to highlight campaigns, programs, and promotions on a regular basis. The option to feature a paid influencer instead of their employees was available. But if you're considering that switch, ask yourself a few questions about the Best Buy example:

- Would a paid influencer have fixed Best Buy's employee engagement issues in the same way?

- Could a paid influencer educate and inform customers with content, or the same level of authentic expertise as the "Blue Shirt" team?
- Could a paid influencer build relationships by allowing customers to experience the brand's personality in the same way?

The easy answer to every one of these questions is *absolutely not*. The real influence had to come from within.

Team members are influence all-stars who are not driven by a contract. They don't have a list of engagement goals, and successful conversion rates aren't their primary motivation for supporting the company's story. Just regular employees proud of the brand they represent and volunteer to join in the celebration of the story. They can speak straight from the heart when supporting the brand. Their collective participation makes a far greater impact because their message is authentic, real, and relatable. Human beings tend to trust the other human beings in their community and "tribe" when it comes to making purchase decisions.

Brands have an unprecedented opportunity to coordinate associations with authentic, integrated influencers of every type to design an engine of influence geared toward brand story education and celebration. My term for this more inclusive influencer—the one who truly matters most—is a **Brand Celebrator**.

Celebrators aren't scripted supporters. They are influencers who elevate brands through their real

Great musicians don't force themselves to read notes. They feel the music. They relax and become part of it.

Celebrators don't force themselves to participate. They feel the brand's story. They relax and become part of it.

relationships with them. Celebrators know that their participation in the brand's story is not only welcome, but valued, encouraged, and meaningful. This confidence and support inspires them to freely participate, and gives them the ability to contribute openly, fearlessly, and authentically.

The difference is similar to a gifted musician who is given a sheet of music. If you hand the musician the sheet and then provide them with detailed instructions on how to play the notes in a specific way, the music might sound good, but it won't be great. However, if you present the same sheet music to the same musician, allow them to take in the sound, and encourage them to create their own version, the music will stand out as an inspired rendition.

Participation becomes more influential and inspiring when people can inject their own ideas and emotions. This type of support isn't mandated or memorized; it's authentic and original. This freedom inspires unique content, ideas, and innovations to flow, elevating your company above the noise and attention grabbing.

Whether an employee writing a post or interacting with a customer, a community partner spreading the word, or a longtime customer referring your business regularly, authentic brand celebrators are your influencer all-stars. They add power to your voice, help you gain trust, and build credibility in your message. The best news is that you can inspire Celebrator-level participation from individuals as well as groups, and they all work together to form an engine of influence.

Celebrators add their own unique perspectives, ideas, and interpretations. Their contributions keep the brand from becoming stagnant by continually creating inspired renditions of the story. The impact of these associations is what moves the brand forward, gains more attention for the brand, and helps your story progress.

Over the last decade, the team at Brand Story Experts and I have specialized in our process, and we have helped our customers celebrate their stories to well over 100 markets, reaching out to hundreds of millions of customers. This resource works, and you will understand the difference between an authentic story and an imitation after reading this book.

I look forward to your progress on this exploration. Read on for some ways to reach out and continue your journey to fully understanding the opportunity to celebrate your story.

SUMMARY:

- Every business in this era needs to acknowledge, understand, and pursue influencers, but the story has to be right and the influencer relationship has to be believable.

- An influencer only matters and makes sense for the brand if they possess the ability to be attached to or engaged with the brand's story in a real and relatable way.

- The best influencer relationships are built on integration, alignment, and shared values. Brands need to look beyond the number of followers an influencer has and consider their authenticity before anything else.

- The opportunity to step up and be an influencer, to impact a brand's story and create change, is open to everyone.

CHAPTER TWO

Celebrating > Telling

IT NEVER FAILS. Approach a company leader and ask them what makes their company great and they all say the same things:

"It's our people."

"It's our service."

"It's our quality."

And, sure, to some degree these statements are true. But as they say in *Game of Thrones*: "Words are wind." In a lot of cases, it's a boring wind that doesn't inspire anyone.

If you're the only one talking about yourself, is this a good sign for your business?

As we continue, we will elevate your understanding of marketing so you don't have to do all the work. You will have more tools than simply competing on price, and you won't have to say the same things everyone else is saying. **Your journey will highlight the differences between telling and celebrating your business, your brand, your work, and your commitment.**

To have the company you've always wanted and to have the influence that was always possible, you just need to access the resources all around you—from the strengths in your story to the people positioned to deliver your work.

It's a matter of getting Positive, Powerful, and Purposeful® about the opportunity around us.

Are you ready to turn your business into a celebration? To have what you've dreamed of?

Great! We're going to show you exactly what's possible.

First, just understand this core idea:

—

THE DIFFERENCE BETWEEN TELLING AND CELEBRATING YOUR BRAND STORY IS AS CRYSTAL CLEAR AS THE DIFFERENCE BETWEEN A PARTY AND A LECTURE.

—

Most people have been lectured to at some point in their lives. A boss, a teacher, or our parents have all "sat us down" to deliver some information. And, look, when you have to deliver a lot of content, a lecture can work. But rarely are people inspired by a lecture. We certainly don't invite others to come and be part of one.

People are *inspired* to join a party.

A party is inviting and interactive. It's effortless.

And it's fun.

But nobody will ever want to listen to a lecture about your brand. To really spread the message, you have to stop telling your story and start celebrating it by making it a party.

This chapter will share how to do that. The goal is to create a culture-defining shift to inspire an army of supporters to join in your story celebration.

It's a transformational opportunity that will help you inspire others, generate excitement, and build something meaningful. To forge a brand story celebration, you have to get people interested, excited, and integrated with the brand. They can't lean against the wall at the edge of the room and watch the party. A wallflower is not an influencer, and they certainly aren't a Celebrator.

Brand celebrators will lead by example, but they must have the freedom to move in their own way. Instead of forcing a narrative, the environment is set up so it's easy for people to get involved on their own terms. When you visualize a great party you don't see everyone doing the same thing. The scene is welcoming and inviting, offering diverse opportunities for different people to get into the mix.

- The flashy ones are on the dance floor showing their moves.
- The comedians share stories and tell jokes.
- The active attendees are playing cornhole outside and enjoying the weather.
- The foodies taste the tapas and enjoy the wine.
- Some partygoers are in seclusion, perfectly happy just being there, texting pictures to their friends and saying, "Look at the good time I'm having!"

All attendees contribute to the party in different ways, which is the beauty of a brand story celebration. Participation will range from amped up to energized to intellectually engaged. The party enhances the experience through the unique sharing of perspectives, insights, and ideas. The good news is that all of this energy is transferable because celebrators emit authentic emotion.

—

PEOPLE PICK UP ON IT. LIKE-MINDED INDIVIDUALS ARE DRAWN TO IT. THEY CONNECT WITH IT. AND THEY BEGIN TO FEEL THE VIBE.

—

When you move from "telling" your story to "celebrating" your story, you intensify and multiply your message. With more people involved, the narrative becomes much more than one voice and one vision. The opportunity becomes available for increased input, more robust support, and more considerable influence. You also set your company up for long-term success with a strategy that continually evolves through an influx of participation and influence.

Stop planning and plotting to "tell" your story.

PEOPLE LOVE RELATIONSHIPS, NOT TRANSACTIONS

There is a very distinct contrast between story-telling and story-celebration. Let's clarify the separation so you'll be able to easily understand and remember the difference.

TELLING YOUR STORY

Brand storytelling is a sharing style where brand leaders assert themselves as the dominant speaker, steering the story toward sales and conversions.

Telling your story is a transactional approach to sharing your story.
It's a Tell-to-Sell strategy.

The brand knows where they want the narrative to go, and they drive it there. Through this approach, brand leadership selectively shares the information and ideas they want to reinforce, and they direct the story. The brand tells people what they want them to know, and takes them where they want them to go.

Nobody is inspired by this tactic.

The deliberate strategy of telling your story provides greater control of the messaging and the ability to create short-term target outcomes. When you Tell-to-Sell, you focus on creating impulse attachments, quick actions, and conversions. The problem is it results in diminishing returns. You can only tell so often, and when you do it forcibly, the public isn't inspired to pass on that message.

CELEBRATING YOUR STORY

A Brand story celebration is a sharing style where the brand invites and encourages everyone to take part in creating a joint narrative centered on brand story education.

Celebrating your story is an interactive approach to sharing your story.
It is a Celebrate-to-Educate strategy.

The brand prioritizes sharing content that educates to initiate awareness, increase understanding, and build long-term relationships. The goal is to motivate like-minded persons to integrate their interests, personality, and perspective with the narrative. The co-creative process inspires them to take part in sharing and celebrating their version of the story, merging their input and ideas with the brand's message.

When you commit to celebrating your story, you do give up a little bit of executive control. But, in return, you gain a brand that can grow on its own. A brand story celebration creates new and supportive social capital. When supporters are actively engaged in content collaboration, the support continually injects new energy and ideas into the brand. The story doesn't stop—it becomes fluid and continues.

Co-creation expands the message, multiplies the connection points, and increases the opportunities for partnering, teaming, collaborating, innovating, educating, and influencing.

The "Celebrating > Telling" comparison makes it easy for any business leader to realize that celebrating is a far greater method of sharing your brand story. Companies need to let go of the fear of losing control of the story and embrace the shift from telling to celebrating their story. Your story celebration is an ongoing, interactive narrative that informs, educates, and inspires consumers about your business. It is fueled by the power of participation, which is the secret to setting your brand up for long-term success through a growing, smiling "army" of influencers.

THE ELEMENTS OF A BRAND CELEBRATION

Everyone wants this army of influencers. Everyone wants their brand to have a vision and dream of a common goal. But how do we establish this type of brand celebration?

—

START WITH THE TRUTH.

—

Your brand celebration is more like sculpting than pottery. Take what's already true about the way you operate and **reveal** it, rather than making something out of nothing. You don't "fake it until you make it." You have to start with your truth and elevate it.

> *Every block of stone has a statue inside it and it is*
> *the task of the sculptor to discover it.*
>
> ~ MICHELANGELO

Every company has values that it has a natural inclination toward. For some businesses, speedy delivery is most important. For others, a close link to a charity is critical. In both cases, the brand promise has to be true. If you pretend that a cat is a dog, people will figure it out when the cat doesn't bark. Tell the truth about the way your brand operates, and double down on the values that you possess and deliver.

Get Clarity: Clearly define who you really are and what you naturally believe in. How you show up and how you make a first impression on people is a collaborative effort between your current actions and how your existing market relates to you.

Learn What Inspires Others: In every single business—no matter how "boring"—there are aspects of their story that will inspire. Nobody will ever claim that Little Caesars makes the best pizza in the world. But they have good pizza for a great price that's ready to go right now. People respect the fact that Little Caesars owns that story, and that's enough for people to spread the word.

Emphasize It Internally: The most important audience for a brand today is the internal one. A story celebration starts inside a business and resonates outward. Uncovering the truths about your brand and celebrating with pride who you are will cultivate a story celebration filled with trust—one that molds employee behavior and transitions your story into a collective force. Remember, this engine of influence starts from within.

Organizational leadership must strongly value the opportunity and make a plan to emphasize your story internally before you release it externally. When leadership stresses the story to the team, that group is influenced and inspired and the story beams from inside. The community and your customers will see the light, and they will be inspired by it too. A true, scintillating story creates common ground, develops a sense of pride, and gains stronger relationships built on trust and appreciation. These connections set you up for long-term success by endowing you with the strength and resiliency needed to navigate changes and challenges in the future.

OVERCOMING CHALLENGE THROUGH CELEBRATION

The power of a brand celebration is that if you do it correctly, you can ride the wave through the most challenging times. The following two businesses had to face different challenges: One faced massive layoffs that crippled a community. The other had to weather an ethics scandal that rocked their business to its core.

HIUT: RESPONDING TO AN EXTERNAL CRISIS

In 2002, 10 percent of the population of Cardigan, Wales, lost their jobs. The country's largest jean factory outsourced the local denim production to Morocco. The town was devastated.

Cardigan natives and apparel veterans David and Clare Hieatt had a vision to build a company that would restore lost jobs and bring the community's soul back to Cardigan. They started the Hiut Denim Company, rehired the original team, and began celebrating. The story is that these 400 team members are the world's most talented jeans makers, focused solely on making the world's best jeans. It's a simple celebration, but it had a profound effect.

Hiut Denim Company's brand story celebration is simple and direct, but also comprehensive.

- Constructed around the commitment, passion, and skill of their team
- Focuses on illustrating the uniqueness of their artistic, handmade process
- Proudly promotes their results by showcasing the world's best jeans

They are emphatically educating people about the skill and mastery of the team. They even call their most experienced jeans makers **Grand Masters**. David uses this term because he "wants to celebrate them as makers."

This style of celebration not only appeals to consumers, but it builds pride and participation. The team members have become influencers. Showcased through social channels and featured on the website, they even sign the jeans they create. This much participation and integration will make anyone with a heart and respect for hard work a Hiut Denim Company fan.

Hiut Denim's motto, "Do one thing well," references their sole focus on making jeans. Clearly, trying to be all things to all people is not their goal. They keep their story celebration simple. Too often, brands attempt to encompass too much and end up accomplishing little. While Hiut Jeans successfully focuses on doing one thing well, they champion their story consistently in many ways. Let's take a look at just a few of them.

- **Simple but Memorable Story Videos:** Videos are tremendous brand story tools, and Hiut Denim clearly realizes this. Videos educate the public, connect them with their people, and allow them to feel their passion.

- **An Absolutely Killer Email Newsletter:** It builds relationships by consistently updating their story through factory news, photographs, information about product innovations, fashion tips, and even provides product discounts.

- **A Perfectly Matched Website:** The design is simple and stylish, providing an ideal setting for inspiring education about their story, skill, quality, and people.

- **Clever and Heartfelt Social Media:** The content represents the brand's image and style perfectly. They share plenty of well-crafted educational material on their people, their mindset, and their commitment to get #OnePercentBetter each day.

- **A Unique Company Yearbook:** Each published version is uncommonly different and furnishes a cool way to remember the past, to see their progress, and to celebrate their people.

It showcases evolution and innovation to recap history in the making.

The Hiut Denim Company story grows because they give people the freedom to celebrate the company's story in their own way. Participation in the celebration is invited; they don't demand it. Praise is publicized for those who want to get their ideas out there, to change things, and make a difference. Creating a celebration-driven culture is ideal brand story leadership.

This type of support opens the door for influential participation from team members, customers, suppliers, Cardigan residents, and more. Even celebrities join in. Yes, when former Duchess Meghan Markle visited the village of Cardiff for an official visit with her husband, Prince Harry, she wore a pair of Hiut Denim Company's black jeans. The power of influence reached new heights.

Markle knew the Hiut Denim Company story, and she was participating in its celebration. People took notice.

Markle's support caused such a surge in demand that the tiny company was forced to move to a bigger factory to cope with a three-month backlog of orders. They called it "The Meghan Effect." In truth, Markle is just one more person celebrating the story, and the Welsh-based brand could not have hoped for a more powerful Celebrator.

The story got so big that e-commerce leader Shopify posted a video that features the Hiut Denim Company story on YouTube and titled it "The Denim Company Who Makes Meghan Markle's Jeans." As the company began to build recognition as "the jeans that Meghan Markle wears," owner David Hieatt illustrated his pride and confidence in knowing that the celebration of his team and company would continue.

"These people are world-class at what they do, and suddenly people are taking them seriously, and yeah, they are fucking good at what they do and let's celebrate it."

I love that quote. David makes it crystal clear that they aren't telling a story—they are celebrating their story, and they are fired up about it.

The important thing to notice is that Meghan Markle's influence wasn't the reason Hiut exploded. They were ready to blow up. They had a true story, true quality, and a spectacular product. Without those things firmly in place, no brand endorsement would have made much of a difference.

Now we can take a look at how celebrating—and owning—the truth can bring a company out of a crisis, even one they invented.

VOLKSWAGEN: RESPONDING TO AN INTERNAL CRISIS OF THEIR OWN DESIGN

Every company will make big mistakes at some point. A misguided service experience will go viral, you might errantly hire a person who ends up catastrophically affecting your culture, or your response to regulatory and ethical challenges could be poor. Challenges like these just happen. Hopefully, your business will never make a mistake as big as Volkswagen, but if you do, you'll see that a celebration can see you through.

On December 10, 2015, Volkswagen Chairman Hans-Dieter Pötsch made a public admission that a group of Volkswagen engineers had decided to cheat on emissions tests in 2005. They were unable to find a technical solution within the company's "time frame and budget" to build diesel engines that would meet US emissions standards.

This emissions scandal sent Volkswagen into a tailspin. The brand was criticized, mocked, and scolded everywhere. The company faced a tough challenge regarding the celebration of their story. They were forced to answer the question: "What do you do when the party gets ugly?" For them, the answer was that the best course of action was to pause, regroup, and then restart the celebration when they had a plan.

When your story suffers a blow like this, the best way to move forward is to acknowledge the disconnect that occurred, assess the reputation that remains, and plan to restart the celebration, as Volkswagen did.

Their first video to address the scandal was right on target. It was 1 minute and 45 seconds long, and titled "Hello Light." It begins with a Volkswagen engineer opening a door and walking into a pitch-black building. As he enters, you hear audio snippets of news reports of the 2015 scandal. You hear the engineer flip off the news reports, and the screen goes dark for nearly 5 seconds before a single desk light comes on. The engineer looks frustrated, almost defeated.

As he moves out of the frame, the Simon & Garfunkel classic "The Sound of Silence" begins to play. Coming back into frame, the engineer sits and starts to sketch, working in the dimly lit setting. He walks up to a light board featuring old drawings of VW's classic Microbus and is inspired. The music kicks up as team members join in. Planning is shown, technology appears, manufacturing is happening, and then a set of lit headlights unveil ... the new electric VW Microbus drives out of the shadows. The ad ends with the on-screen declaration: "In the darkness, we found the light. Introducing a new era of electric driving."

VW was back in brand story celebration mode with the Microbus in a starring role. This story asset acted as an incredible influencer. It brought back positive, nostalgic memories of the past while also promoting a promising future. Even though the electric version of the Microbus isn't set to arrive until 2022, it made perfect sense as an Influencer. (See the video at EveryoneIsAnInfluencer.com/VW.)

This wasn't a campaign to sell the VW Microbus, and the content wasn't being shared to fix a sales problem. They had a story problem and needed to grab control of the story and steer the narrative back to the most inspiring aspects of their brand. They needed to restart their brand story celebration.

This storyline campaign was designed to reenergize the brand and regain some positive momentum. They followed the "Hello Light" video with a series of aligned print ads. The headline for one was "After the bad buzz, here's a better one." On-brand copywriting combined the cool VW bus vibe of the past with a promise for the future.

The presentation of "Hello Light" opened the door to talk about the company's drive to be the leading electric car company in the world. The conversation involved the environment, social responsibility, and community responsibility, which masterfully evolved their VW story celebration.

In June 2019, VW took the evolution of their story celebration process even further as the company released a press release statement on their US Media site announcing its new shift to "Drive Bigger." Volkswagen of America Senior Vice President of Marketing Jim Zabel said this message was designed to "become a touchstone for the company, amplifying the work of the people and organizations who make positive contributions to their communities." Again, they weren't selling cars. They were educating people about their story in the hope they would inspire individuals who felt the same way to be a part of something bigger than themselves.

Zabel drove that point home by saying, "Drive Bigger goes way beyond a traditional ad campaign. It is a public declaration of a long-term vision for Volkswagen that calls to a higher purpose and challenges us all, Volkswagen very much included, to move beyond just self-interest and to consider something bigger."

The statement illustrates Volkswagen's commitment to driving their story past self-appreciation and into passionate participation, where people attach themselves to the brand based on a larger goal. He cements this objective by saying, "In a time where the world has long catered to self-interest, we will invite people to see a more progressive path. It's a point of view we're dedicated to as we look to the future, and it's a belief we can champion as we evolve our values in classic Volkswagen style: with humility, humanity, and humor."

Great stuff. Great rebound. Great story.

BRAND CELEBRATION SUMMARY

Every brand story is different, and that's a good thing. Brands have the freedom to develop and execute their own unique strategy for celebration. Hiut Denim and VW are valuable examples of companies who are thriving and surviving through a brand story celebration strategy that works for them.

Executing a story strategy that celebrates who you are isn't easy. Challenges and choices will complicate the process. Next we will examine some of these instances while discussing the mindset needed to generate and execute an effective brand story celebration.

SUMMARY: ─────────────────────────

- A brand celebration needs people who are interested, excited, and integrated with your brand.

- A brand celebration requires that you: get clarity, tell the truth, learn what your inclinations are, and then learn where your community picks up on that. Then you reinforce the best parts internally.

- Find the real things that matter and elevate them to attract people who are also interested in them.

- Get excited—life is too short not to celebrate stories.

CHAPTER THREE

Honesty Is No Longer Optional

IN THE LAST chapter, we talked about how honesty is a mandatory building block for every brand celebration. In today's world, it's not just "nice to have"; it's a necessary condition for survival. If people come to a party full of fakes, they're not likely to stay ... and they certainly won't come back.

The party metaphor emphasizes the social support needed to grow beyond a lifeless, one-sided lecture to gain brand story participation. Brand story development isn't a one-person party driven by a single brand perspective. It's social, energetic, engaging, and interactive. The brand has a voice. The customers have a voice, and your vendors have a voice.

—

SOCIAL MEDIA IS YOUR INVITATION TO A PARTY THAT NEVER ENDS.

—

Content marketing and social media marketing are the modern way of creating an open invitation for similar people to join your celebration. Influencers have to be in the game to educate and inspire, so a good host makes it easy for them to find their way into the story and get involved.

The goal is to create an **engine of influence** where your most passionate supporters have—and exercise—the opportunity to celebrate your story in concert together.

The examples of Hiut Jeans and VW demonstrate that it's not enough to have a good idea. You need *real* commitment and ongoing support. Business leaders encouraging their team members to celebrate as a team will recognize and reward their participation. It is important to celebrate wins and get excited about showing your own team, who your company is, and how the team can execute on your brand promises.

To gain internal participation, team members need to feel good about educating others on the brand's story by posting their accomplishments, showing their pride, and sharing their experiences. This builds integrated relationships with customers and clients while solidifying and strengthening the structure of your business. It embraces the opportunity to celebrate your story to initiate a stronger culture and company.

Influence without integration is meaningless. A brand can get a big voice, but if you suddenly started telling the public inconsistent facts, it would fall apart. Kenyan long-distance runner Eliud Kipchoge endorsed Nike's Air Zoom Alpha Fly Next% shoe. He broke the two-hour-marathon world record in 2019 wearing the shoe, creating one of Nike's biggest selling (and most controversial) shoes ever. The impact of his influencer relationship with Nike's shoe is undeniable.

But if Krispy Kreme saw this success and then hired Eliud to promote their donuts, the campaign would most likely fall flat. When you want to leverage influence in your business, a clear understanding of who you really are is required. Partnering with a "non-integrated" influencer will cause problems.

THE RUBY SLIPPERS ARE RIGHT HERE, DOROTHY

This book appealed to you because chances are, something doesn't feel right at your company. At the very least, you are searching for some ideas or insight to make things better. Maybe it's gotten hard to acquire new customers, and even harder to keep existing ones. Keeping your *employees* can be just as tricky. Everyone is fighting for the right customers and team members in this full-scale battle. To step up and help your company be distinct, you can't roll out a tired, overused marketing strategy.

The good news is that you already have what is required to build a strong culture through communication and collaboration. You've already earned this tool—you just need to uncover and deploy it. Yes, everything you need to educate, to relate, to build influence, and to win is centered on the single most important asset that every brand possesses—the opportunity to celebrate your story.

Your *story* is the answer.

THE TIME IS NOW, BUT THERE ARE NO SHORTCUTS

The ability for businesses to communicate their story is far greater today than any other time in history. The problem isn't that companies aren't recognizing the opportunity, but that businesses and brands are trying to take shortcuts.

Some brands do this intentionally, while many others do it unintentionally. Either way, it's easy to understand how these missteps occur.

A decade ago, it became evident that the internet provided an incredible opportunity for brands to share their story. Marketing Departments lit up with excitement, jumping at the chance to tell their brand's story.

They immediately started writing copy and making brand story–type videos, most of which turned into clichés. They neglected to spend the necessary time to uncover the story, and they simply started telling. They thought the public would watch and be interested just because they spent big bucks on a cinema camera and the video looked professional.

Nobody cared.

The brands misfired because they were telling their story without a proven process: no supporting storylines and no commitment to celebrating their story. No process to create a culture shift had been developed—they were simply selling a story. As a result, these Tell-to-Sell brand stories were recognized as self-serving, failing to inspire or produce a positive impact.

—

DON'T BE A BRAND THAT
JUST TELLS STORIES.

—

The opportunity to share stories still existed, but instead of figuring out a way to handle brand stories correctly, story marketing frameworks emerged, illustrating how brands could take an easier, quicker route. "Avoid taking the time to tell brand stories and instead be a brand who tells stories." It is a pure Tell-to-Sell strategy, with a version of your brand story that is designed to convert not educate. Most of this guidance was built around traditional storytelling principles.

Here are a few of the recommended strategies that may sound familiar:

- Don't make your story about you.

- Invite customers to be a part of "a" story, not your story.

- Illustrate how your product or service makes the customer a hero.

- Make the main message about what's in it for the consumer.

These are just a few of the widespread principles that companies began implementing to capitalize on the opportunity to tell stories. The ideas are sound sales strategies: "Better than average" tactics to create connections and quick conversions through copywriting. But they shouldn't be the main strategy that you employ. Telling stories that aren't connected to brand education may gain attention but they only provide surface-level connections. They don't build relationships, differentiate your business, or set you up for long-term success. Telling stories is a sharing process that does not have the transformational power of a story celebration. Story Telling is a short-term tactic. Story Celebration is a long-term strategy.

> Story Telling is a short-term tactic. Story Celebration is a long-term strategy.

Your story celebration opens up the opportunity to share stories that stand out. Instead of recycling customer hero concepts and regurgitating the same narrative as your competitors, look for fresh and unique stories inside of your company and your culture. Highlight your team, your customers, or your community in ways that educate people with real-life, relatable extensions of your story.

Lead by example and make an effort to inspire others to share stories in this manner as well. There are endless opportunities to celebrate your story in a way that is compelling and inclusive. When you make it easy for everyone to understand the story you are celebrating, influential examples will begin to emerge all around you.

If you want to take advantage of the opportunity to celebrate your story to build your culture and establish long-term relations, you have to clarify—then celebrate—who you really are. No shortcuts.

Ten years ago, Tell-to-Sell storytelling strategies worked consistently to form impulse connections. The stories did well because few companies were telling stories at all. Now, the Tell-to-Sell game is played out. The public is tired of seeing the same stories over and over again. Story burnout is happening faster than ever.

During the first few weeks of the COVID-19 pandemic, people were inspired by brands relaying the message, "We're in This Together," as it seemed heartfelt and timely. However, it didn't take long for all types of brands to jump on board with this storytelling strategy. Soon there was an explosion of nearly identical narratives. The story shifted from inspiring to annoying.

One surprising brand created a clever reversal on the overplayed "We're in This Together" by "Leaning In" to who they really were. The response came through hundreds of comments and thousands of likes. Steak-umm, a brand of Quaker Maid Meats, got tons of Twitter engagement with humorous but honest replies like this:

Templated ideas, or a ready-made brand strategy, are definitely not recommended. When your story is designed around who you think you need to be to compete, you are left with inauthentic, surface-level storylines that blend in with everyone else.

—

THE PRICE OF FAKE IS DEATH.

—

We've talked about the perils of shortcutting the process through shallow Tell-to-Sell storytelling; however, what's worse yet is pretending to be something that you're not. If you are looking to build long-term relationships, make sure that your brand story represents a story that you can live up to and execute.

Your authentic brand story elevates your brand. When your message is real and relatable, you separate yourself from the imitators and wannabe brands. This separation is not a luxury but a necessity.

It is fatal for brands to be phony. Too many of those games are played and people want relief. They're tired of duplicated stories, fake news, counterfeit reviews, retargeting games, and highly questionable sources. Deceptive practices have been so disruptive that the *New York Times* referred to the 2010s as the "Decade of Mistrust" in the final *Sunday Review* of 2019. They suggested that the decade's biggest lesson was **"Americans learned that they shouldn't trust anyone or anything."**

—

CUSTOMERS ARE LONGING FOR CONTENT THEY CAN TRUST.

—

Customers are forced to search for sources they can trust and reviews they can believe in. That struggle is real, and the shift has impacted the reputation, relevancy, and value of social channels. These channels have the most to lose if the confidence, value, and validity of their platforms continue to diminish.

Google, Facebook, LinkedIn, Yelp, and every other successful social platform are constantly evolving to address the effect of trust issues and content concerns. They know that their platform can only stay relevant as long as they remain trusted, useful, and engaging.

These companies cannot afford to sit back as the fakers and phonies halt their momentum—too much is at stake. So the fight is on, more successfully in some places than others. Each site battles daily to defend their community and reputation by perfecting their own algorithms, which will produce and protect the most trusted results and compelling content possible.

- Google continually updates its algorithm to ensure the most relevant search results based on content that people use. They have penalized companies for keyword games, link schemes, sneaky redirects, automatically generated content, and any other questionable practice that would be considered a search engine scam. This commitment is a direct reflection of how much they value the user experience.

- Facebook gave its algorithm a massive overhaul in January 2018, and they continue to enforce strict safeguard policies by punishing clickbait, spammers, and game players. They clearly are committed to prioritizing family, friends, and genuine stories. They value likes, comments, and shares more than ever, and they pay attention to the brands that users interact with often.

- Yelp realized the threat of fake reviews early on. In 2012, they learned that at least 20–25 percent of their reviews were suspicious. They took drastic measures and adjusted their algorithms to scrutinize reviews heavily for authenticity. However, many business owners feel that far too many authentic reviews are unfairly tossed aside in the approval process. Yelp is still struggling to find the right balance.

These are only a fraction of the actions being taken to protect the value and trust of online messaging. Any social channel that has survived and thrived over the past decade has done so because they have spent an enormous amount of time creating and implementing a strategy for keeping their content engaging and authentic. They know that for their channels to build a trusted environment, the information needs to do more than just exist. Channels need to be a source to educate and entertain people through authentic influence.

Whether it's making sure that you get the perfect Google result or ensuring that you are targeted with valuable memories on Facebook, social channels are focused on delivering content their users care about. It is in their best interest to connect users to companies, products, and experiences that they value.

Every step in the direction of quality content and brand story accountability clears up the clutter. It also puts the spotlight on brands that have benefited from manipulating the system. This new era of accountability in storytelling shines a light on deceptive companies, manipulators, and shady marketers. It's a shift for the good, as there are few things worse than a brand that positions itself as something it isn't.

DON'T TALK SHIT UNLESS ...

My distaste for brands that take shortcuts was cemented into my psyche at a young age.

I was raised in Steubenville, Ohio, by parents who both had doctorates in education. They gave their children sound morals, a strong work ethic, and a desire to excel in life. Through all their guidance and support, one principle stood out as a compass that helped me navigate academics, athletics, business, and life.

It was a simple rule:

—

DON'T TALK SHIT IF
YOU CAN'T BACK IT UP.

—

Obviously my dad didn't invent this phrase. I'm sure you've heard someone say something like it. For us, it wasn't just a saying. In the Keenan household, it was an actual rule. My brothers and I knew that a person simply did not talk about doing, being, or having something unless they were prepared to back it up.

Hearing this rule over and over trained me to despise the idea of misrepresenting myself and my accomplishments. This mindset not only helped me grow through accountability, but it taught me to take pride in the person I was becoming.

Unfortunately, once I was out in the working world, it didn't take long to realize that not everyone chose to bite their tongue when it came to shit-talking. I was shocked to see how prominently misrepresentations from this type of talk loomed in the culture of companies. This was before the advent of the internet and accountable marketing, so companies who regularly lied or misrepresented themselves faced few real consequences when they failed to back up their promises. Aside from the occasional negative review in *Consumer Reports*, buyers didn't have access to the information required to hold these organizations accountable.

Today, a company who regularly talks shit will eventually lose big-time. When a brand sets expectations that it can't or won't meet, reality bites back in the form of negative ratings and reviews. A business may escape public notice at first, but it is courting the real possibility of severe repercussions for failing to deliver the promoted expectations. A brand can't be positioned for success in the future if its story is not authentic.

Review sites and other web-based forums may be battling authenticity issues, but the overall rankings earned by brands still carry enormous weight and influence. That accountability has put companies on trial in the court of public opinion. When you fake it till you make it, the public can be a harsh judge. For that reason, it is more important than ever for businesses to be who they are and avoid talking shit.

THIS IS FOR PEOPLE WHO DELIVER.

If your company can deliver on its promise to employees and customers, your enthusiasm about this new era of accountability will spread. Reading this book shows you're ready and willing to supply even better ways to fulfill the promise of your brand story. We're not talking about becoming slaves to every consumer whim—you can't be all things to all people. The flip side of accountability is the power to greatly amplify the inspirational aspects of your company.

Now that our discussion has covered the evolution and emergence of authenticity, the next section moves on to discuss how to share your brand story in celebratory fashion through a process that we call Culture Development Marketing (CDM). This system educates supporters, solidifies your values, and strengthens your culture through different versions and visions of your brand's story. Integration and involvement are the ultimate activators for helping brands stand out and succeed.

SUMMARY:

- Honesty is vital. People will figure it out quickly if you're not.

- You have to use honest methods: Google, Facebook, and Yelp are rapidly deploying algorithmic methods to weed out the fakes. Stay on the right side of the street.

- You can't talk shit. People are looking for content and individuals they can trust and believe in. Only talk about the things that you do naturally.

CHAPTER FOUR

Culture Development Marketing

J AIME DIDOMENICO WAS skeptical. His company was one of the biggest successes in its market in 2009, but there was something missing from his marketing. I was pitching him a radical change—something different—and I wasn't sure he was up for it.

My agency had just relaunched. We presented our new, exclusive process of Culture Development Marketing to Jaime for his company, CoolToday. This exceptional home service company employed great people and was earning under $10 million in revenue at that time in the heating, ventilation, and air conditioning (HVAC) industry. However, as CoolToday grew beyond HVAC, their growth shaped two additional brands: PlumbingToday, for plumbing, and EnergyToday, for electrical. The non-cohesive structure of the three brands caused issues internally and externally.

CoolToday's success was fueled by a robust media plan, as Jaime was one of the top advertisers in his market. However, the lion's share of their messaging was all about the CoolToday brand. Even the company's jingle was all about HVAC. The catchy and memorable tune reinforced the strong value statement "CoolToday or You Don't Pay." But having a jingle that only marketed the company's HVAC brand was, in part, contributing to their business issues.

When I met with Jamie, I instantly saw that he was a bright, intelligent leader who valued his people and culture. He began the meeting by saying, "A previous ad agency I met with told me that our CoolToday, PlumbingToday, and EnergyToday brands were a problem." I asked what their solution was, and he said, "No solutions were offered. They just said, 'You've got a problem.'"

Normally, a statement like this would be concerning. However, the closer I looked into his business, I didn't see a problem but an opportunity. This type of situation was well suited for our process. In fact, he'd be an ideal client, so I took a chance.

I disagreed with the other agency, feeling that CDM could help him bring it all together to create one comprehensive and compelling narrative. The ability to define a clear, cohesive story would allow him to celebrate his team and customer relationships in a way that went far beyond the usual advertising of tune-ups, drain clearings, and electric panel inspections.

Of course, he had no clue what CDM was. Rightfully so, as it was a process that we had just begun unveiling.

Before he kicked me out of his office, I asked, "What if there was a process to allow everyone to understand the brand as a whole?"

He perked up because he had thought of his company as one thing. I explained how we could uncover the story of the winning culture that already existed in his company. The celebration of this story was just as important *internally* as it was *externally*.

His receptiveness to the idea was immediate. He stopped me midway and said, "You know what I like about this? It gives us a chance to celebrate our people. We need this. Tell me more." His attitude illustrated that he understood the opportunity.

I showed him our one-sentence definition of Culture Development Marketing:

I quickly clarified the statement by explaining that the process worked using the following simple steps:

> Celebrate your Brand Story through ongoing conversations, engagements, and experiences in a way that inspires participation, solidifies your culture, and builds long-term relationships.

- First we do an impression analysis to uncover your brand's most inspiring aspects.

- Then we clarify and connect the ideas through a brand story summary.

- We forge and execute the plan to celebrate that story with your team, customers, and community.

- With a plan set, we check in every year to be certain the storylines remain relevant and that the story is still in order. We will add and remove storylines, characters, and ideas as the needs of your company and community evolve.

CoolToday's customers were already familiar with their reputation for fast service and responsiveness. However, it was clear that they had a lot more to offer than their jingle advertised. CDM was the way to bring that out.

The process would use his team and customers to fuel the celebration. Their participation would help us create user-composed content to support and reinforce the story. Facebook and YouTube would become the main channels used to share photos, spotlight his team, and tell stories. We would produce a series of videos that set their company apart, and our social media team would work hand in hand with his team to build a constant flow of education and understanding.

This content strategy was aimed at advancing relationships. Our goal was to move like-minded people through the following process:

- From Spectators who see the story
- To Appreciators who value the way the story benefits them personally
- To Celebrators who are inspired to take part in the celebration of the story

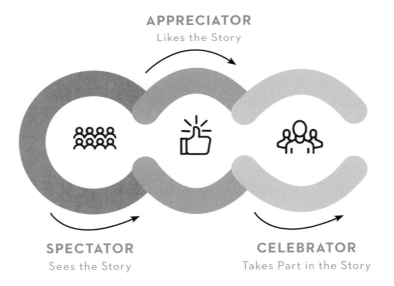

APPRECIATOR
Likes the Story

SPECTATOR
Sees the Story

CELEBRATOR
Takes Part in the Story

For the celebration to last, we needed to establish a story-driven culture where the celebration of the story would become a part of who the company was. Content creation would be a team sport for every department to participate in. Gaining this type of participation from CoolToday, EnergyToday, and PlumbingToday was a game changer.

It was a massive adjustment from their traditional approach. In addition, even though CoolToday's ongoing marketing strategy was being noticed, it was vulnerable to duplication by competitors. Any brand could challenge them based on products, pricing, and a promise of quick response. Now they had the opportunity to bring the story of all three trades together. The CDM process would onboard his entire team and educate people about their company's story through the power of their people.

The more we discussed the opportunity, the more he embraced the idea. He jumped on board, loving the idea of utilizing his team as influencers. He couldn't wait to start the celebration.

DEFINING A NEW DIRECTION

Through the process we uncovered a story that would showcase his team's dedication to taking care of people, helping them to "Get the Best from Today." The story celebration took off.

The plan maintained a focus on timeliness through the word "Today" in a way that made it easy for CoolToday, EnergyToday, and PlumbingToday to commit to brand story education and execution. With all three departments onboard, there were illustrations everywhere. Soon the full-scale celebration featured all the ways the company helped their team, customers, and community to "Get the Best from Today."

The impact was immediate. For the first time, CoolToday, PlumbingToday, and EnergyToday were celebrating their brand story in harmony, in concert with their customers and their community. Together they became a collective force in educating people, illustrating pride in who they were, and asserting themselves. They became story-driven leaders in the home service industry.

STORIES BUILD LONG-TERM SUCCESS

Culture Development Marketing isn't a promotion or a temporary program—it's a cultural commitment to getting long-term results. More than a decade later, the CoolToday story grows, evolves, and continues to be celebrated. In fact, they have celebrated their story so effectively that they have grown to over $50 million in revenue. They dominate in their competitive home service market and are consistently recognized as leaders in the industry.

CDM can be the ultimate difference-maker, value-builder, and trust-generator. We continue to have success with CoolToday and dozens of other home service companies. While the results and successes may be similar for these companies, the story is never the same. Every company's story is unique, and it elevates their brand because their plan is built around celebrating who they are.

Brands who commit to celebrating their authentic brand story are doing more than advertising. They are giving consumers what they want: real information, real content, and the real story about the brand.

—

YOU HAVE TO TRULY KNOW YOUR BRAND
TO TEACH YOUR BRAND.

—

There is a difference between believing that you offer unique personality, results, and benefits and being able to clearly define what those differences are. The goal of summarizing your brand's story is to produce clarity and awareness that sets the framework for your brand celebration.

The process shapes the celebration by forming a story-driven culture:

- Your brand story summary definition initiates a clear understanding of the most inspiring aspects of the brand. It includes the reputation the brand has earned, and it serves as a powerful foundation for content creation.

- Your summary aids in the development of associated storylines that expand the opportunity to celebrate the story. Storylines are subsets of the brand story summary, and each one outlines a key aspect of the brand. These isolated areas open up unified connection opportunities for different groups and personas.

- The brand story celebration happens as the sharing of brand story and storyline content begins to inspire other individuals to take part in content sharing, and creating new stories.

- The insight, ideas, and innovations gained through the sharing of content are the payoff of the party. The exchange keeps a steady flow of education, energy, and excitement funneling through the brand.

- The goal is to construct a story-driven company who keeps the party going.

Through participation in the celebration, "brand-centered content creation" becomes baked into everyday operations. The process expands beyond the idea of brand journalism to create a culture of contribution. Friends, followers, clients, and employees join the celebration with new perspectives, innovative concepts, and valuable input.

MORE THAN CUSTOMERS: YOUR OWN MARKETING ARMY

Once a comprehensive version of your story has been uncovered and is clear, then you construct a plan to promote the story with passion, accuracy, and vigor. The goal of your brand story celebration is to inspire customers, team members, and partners to understand and appreciate your brand on a deeper level. These brand celebrators are the greatest influencer asset for any company.

Inspire as many of these celebrators as possible to become integrated with your narrative. Brand celebrators aren't just loyal customers or advocates who support your brand with their own vision of value. Like-minded people will progress from personal support and understanding of the brand to an integrated relationship with the brand's story.

Like-minded doesn't mean building a brand of clones. Preferences and personalities will ensure that your brand celebrators bond to the brand uniquely. That's the way you want it. Some people like Chick-fil-A for their strong values and some connect with their spicy chicken sandwich. Regardless of the differences in their single perspectives, every Brand Celebrator matters.

When a Celebrator connects with their role in the story, they become your ultimate influencer. They understand and appreciate some part of your story from a perspective that only they possess. Connected through this exclusive vantage point, it allows them to offer one-of-a-kind insight, ideas, and influence.

These people have expectations associated with the experience. They clearly recognize and understand the value it delivers. This awareness is priceless, and it also unlocks their power to be an influencer.

Celebrators have the freedom to bond on their own terms to engage with the brand story, just as they would a favorite movie series, sports team, or community cause. They share in some part of the mission and are able to contribute uniquely in a way that may inspire other amenable people to get involved with the company.

These individuals matter most to the brand itself because their involvement in the brand story celebration at any level provides an opportunity to grow their connections. Brand celebrators want to keep learning. As their insights and understanding grow, they build a comprehensive understanding that enables them to strengthen their own attachment while guiding others toward greater appreciation.

—

THIS CURRICULUM IS FOR EVERYONE.

—

They graduate beyond self-appreciation into a deeper bond with the brand. This type of connection advances a person from a "me" to a "we" mentality. It bonds them with the brand, and the brand is thrilled to have them on board.

It's difficult for many brands to see a messaging strategy as part of anything but marketing. Getting the word out about your story and reinforcing the brand image sound like clear directives for connecting with customers. However, notice that I have been referring to celebrators as **individuals**, not customers or clients. This is intentional because celebrators can be customers, team members, partners, or members of the management team.

The CDM process is designed to increase the connection between brands and enthusiastic people. It is a process designed to reach internal and external individuals, so plan to advance the relationships you have with your team as well. In fact, the first priority in your brand celebration is to onboard your team. Connections begin inside the brand.

Present the story in a way that makes it easy for your team members to see where they fit in. Remember, true influencers are involved and integrated into the story. Team members want to feel included—that their actions and attitude matter. The feeling of inclusion builds pride in their role in making the story happen. This creates a "feedback loop": they tell the story better, they share ideas more often, and they look for ways to celebrate it continually.

When a team member is able to visualize and embrace their role, their value for the work they do increases. Simply gaining personal appreciation is more than enough value for most brands. However, CDM's process pushes further. The goal is that your brand story celebration educates in a way that enables team members to grasp a larger vision of the brand and participate at a greater level.

—

IT'S ALL ABOUT GRADUATION.

—

People long to belong to something bigger than themselves. Customers and team members want to be a part of something that matters more than their own self-interests. It is important that brands look for ways to lead predisposed individuals to learn more and develop a deeper appreciation.

A brand story celebration is more than building excitement and hoopla. It establishes an inclusive environment by driving collaboration, promoting the sharing of knowledge, and creating a culture of contribution.

This deliberate process advances relationships with internal team members or customers to graduate them to a connection level that allows them to understand and appreciate the brand at a new degree. Creating this type of graduation isn't a quick conversion. It's a sustained approach to building long-term relationships.

EDUCATION IS REQUIRED FOR APPRECIATION

The power of content is often undervalued. People see so much content each day that it's overwhelming. Bits of content become useless distractions, so it is easy to understand the lack of appreciation. Disassociated content is senseless and pointless. However, brand story content that ties into a concerted brand story celebration isn't pointless. It is powerful.

Whether it's a social post, a 30-second commercial, or a set of posters that line the halls in your corporate office, purposeful brand story content increases education and support while reinforcing the brand's story. Remember, brand story content is the blood flowing through your organization's celebration. You need educational content to bring your story to life.

When you share content, you freeze the best parts of your brand in time, for all time. For example, featuring a photo of a smiling team member who just received a high-level certification gives you the ability to:

- Inform about the details and importance of the certification
- Explain how the achievement ties to your commitment to training
- Relay your pride in the person who achieved this goal

Just like that, a single piece of content provides an opportunity to tie back to the story, reinforce the storylines, and advance attachment through brand story education. These "high five" moments are great examples of how your brand story celebration inspires through education.

Every piece of content contributes to a continual flow of education. It's a simple sequence required in every brand expression opportunity, and it all adds up to extraordinary results. However, the concept of educating to build understanding and appreciation certainly isn't an exclusive idea to CDM. The principle holds true in almost every relationship.

The more knowledge you have about something, the more opportunities you have to appreciate it on a deeper level. Sports are an excellent illustration of the type of relationship that can be gained when you add education to the celebration.

If you give a person who knows nothing about football perfect seats on the 50-yard line at a frenzied, sold-out NFL game, they won't connect with the game at a deep level. It doesn't matter if the seats are prime, if the crowd is excited, or if the game is a thriller. If they don't understand it, they won't be able to truly get into it.

—

YOU GOTTA KNOW THE GAME TO APPRECIATE IT.

—

Consider the difference if that person who didn't know anything about football were given the tickets for that same game two weeks in advance.

- Soon after, they might become curious about the stadium, so they visit the team's website.

- A retargeting pixel on the team's website tracks their visit to the site and the team extends an invitation to join their Facebook page.

- They "like" the team's page, spend some time there, and learn a little about the team.

- The person sees more ads about the team in their Facebook newsfeed.

- On Facebook, they see pictures of people at the games having a great time. They are introduced to some cool team traditions, and the team recaps events where they helped support the community.

- After a few days, they decide to return to the team's website. They watch some video profiles about a few key players on the team and become motivated to learn more about the team. They watch more short videos about the team's history, the owners, and the fans.

- As the game grows closer, the person visits the team's Instagram page. WOW! They love the photos. They view dozens of images, and in the process they learn that the upcoming game is a rivalry. They hop back over to Facebook and begin interacting with other people on the page to discuss the rivalry and the excitement of attending their first NFL game.

Through the power of the story, this person learned, bonded, and was educated. Now when that "newly educated" fan sits down at that same 50-yard-line seat at the same game, how much more do you think they will value the experience? How much more passionate and involved will this person be? The answer is: a lot.

The point is that if you want to strengthen a story connection, learn more about it. It's that simple. The right education builds interest into appreciation and inspired participation. That same attachment principle applies to the company you work for, the products you use, the services you select, and the activities you choose.

Brand Celebrators are the most influential people to a company because these like-minded people are educated and integrated with your story. They "get" what your organization is all about, proudly celebrate and support what it stands for, and want to be in on the experience. They desire a front-row seat and a T-shirt, and they want to bring their friends to the show, too.

Celebrators continually inject energy and influence into the brand. Their ongoing input and collaboration strengthens the brand, introduces innovative ideas, and keeps the brand progressing through a continual flow of value-building education. Each post, illustration, or example builds influence while infusing your culture with goodwill, positivity, and humanity.

This chapter covered the setup, benefits, and structure of Culture Development Marketing. Now we'll move on to discuss the ingredients needed to make it happen.

SUMMARY:

- Culture Development Marketing requires that you produce content that reflects you at your best.

- Teach your customers AND employees what is "good" so they appreciate you—this is a process.

- Start by uncovering the most inspiring aspects of your company, and then connect them with the "big picture."

- Advance relationships through celebration and education.

CHAPTER FIVE

The Elements of Any Trustworthy Brand

Y OU KNOW THE best way to find out if someone is a Tesla owner? Don't worry, they'll tell you ... right after they tell you about their vegan CrossFit gym.

It's true. Tesla drivers simply cannot help telling everyone they know what they love about their car, and why they are passionate about Tesla. Their connection forms because Tesla continually builds interest education around their story by celebrating it everywhere. They have a powerful, influential narrative because it is clear, authentic, and inclusive. The Tesla brand story introduces similar consumers to something bigger and then invites them to join in and support the cause. They aren't telling a story; they are celebrating a movement.

Tesla is proud of the cars they make, but their uniquely designed products are only one dimension of the story. Their mission statement proudly illustrates that Tesla is more than that:

Tesla's mission is to accelerate the world's transition to sustainable energy. Tesla was founded in 2003 by a group of engineers who wanted to prove that people didn't need to compromise to drive electric—that electric vehicles can be better, quicker, and more fun to drive than gasoline cars.

The brand encourages all comers to be part of something cool, exciting, and meaningful by highlighting the most inspiring aspects of their brand.

HOW TESLA USES BRAND ELEMENTS TO MAKE MEANINGFUL CONNECTIONS

Sharing the Attitude, Drive, and Direction of the brand reveals the elements that people can connect with and trust. Take another look back at the Tesla mission statement to see how it includes Attitude, Drive, and Direction, enabling them to build trust comprehensively.

- **Attitude**: The statement spotlights a positive, proactive perspective in a cool, honest, and exciting way. Tesla's story emits a strong emotional vibe that attracts people, along with the opportunity to align themselves through participation.

- **Drive**: The statement sets up specific connection opportunities by reinforcing their commitment to building cars that are better, quicker, and more fun to drive. That sets the scene to celebrate three areas where Tesla employs concrete systems, habits, and processes to stand out and succeed.

- **Direction**: The statement starts by emphasizing clear direction through operational aspirations, then it raises the stakes by stating that their business is about moving toward an overarching commitment to sustainable energy. They link their brand to meaningful objectives. They can illustrate this through the celebration of the results and the reputation they have earned.

ATTITUDE IS THE EMOTION THAT THE BRAND CARRIES. DRIVE REPRESENTS HOW THE BRAND FUNCTIONS AND OPERATES. DIRECTION IS THE MISSION OF YOUR BRAND.

These areas come together to masterfully create a comprehensive story celebration that is easily understood and appreciated. It sets up expectations associated with the brand's feelings, actions, and interests.

Content creation is easy when you comprehensively uncover an earned narrative and authentic storylines. The ensuing framework constructs a brand celebration that effortlessly guides relationships with enthusiastic people inside and outside a company.

Tesla executes Culture Development Marketing so well that they have gotten to the point where their supporters do all of the heavy lifting for them. The graduation and conversion are nearly effortless.

- From Spectators who are curious to see what Tesla is doing

- To Appreciators who cannot wait to buy the products and ideas that Tesla produces

- To Celebrators who are inspired by the way Tesla designs, acts, and thinks, and are proud to be part of the "Tesla Lifestyle"

Tesla has been able to build this type of bond because success for Tesla isn't about converting a sale: it is about creating an ongoing celebration. Tesla focuses on delivering amazing long-term experiences and builds relationships with excited people inside and outside the brand through the consistent celebration of their story.

Inside, Tesla's team members are energized, quickly identifying their impact and relevance to the mission. Tesla frames this type of connection through clear expectations. An example is the wording of one of their recruitment listings:

Tesla is committed to hiring and developing the top talent in any given discipline. Our world-class teams operate with a product development philosophy, flat organizational structure, and technical contribution at all levels. You will be expected to challenge and be challenged, to create, and to innovate.

That's exciting enough, but then it concludes with: "These jobs are not for everyone." This phrase is like a magnet, attracting people who want to "prove themselves" and fuel Tesla's future success. Everyone at Tesla knows what they are getting themselves into, and they are proud to join. As a result, team members become more engaged and dedicated to the cause, which encourages them to deliver a better customer experience—another feedback loop.

Outside, customers have endless opportunities to establish an inspired connection. From Tesla's **customer-first focus**—that allows purchasing a Tesla to be hassle-free—to a one-of-a-kind referral program where customers can earn valuable rewards through word-of-mouth recommendations. Tesla's experience goes far beyond transactional telling.

Sometimes Elon Musk will log in to a platform and retweet or answer one of his customers, illustrating that he is listening, learning, and interested in hearing what Tesla supporters and celebrators say. This integration with the brand supercharges Elon Musk's influence, because having the opportunity to engage with the company's CEO and founder symbolizes that this guy is "the real thing."

Tesla's brand celebration makes fans feel empowered. They know that their participation and influence are encouraged, appreciated, and valued. Tesla drives the development of this inclusive experience every step of the way. As a result, Tesla owners care about the results of their brand, and are famous for following every move.

Tesla owners are proud of the fact that the company exists to do more than just sell cars. So proud that they do 100 percent of the company's traditional marketing. Yes, Tesla proudly states that they spend $0 on traditional marketing. They even deleted their Facebook page, but their story is so compelling that even without ads, it spreads faster than other brands.

THE RIGHT STORY IS MORE IMPORTANT THAN THE RIGHT CHANNEL.

Tesla stands out with its unique voice—a powerful, unified voice. They aren't "talking at" people, Telling-to-Sell by manipulative customer marketing. They are celebrating the attitude they have, promoting the processes they employ, and shining a light on the difference they are trying to make.

They educate, encourage, and flat out invite others to join the celebration. All of this brand celebration creates a buzz loud enough to initiate the most unique and differentiating marketing possible—with no advertising costs. Here are just a few of the ways that Tesla gains a tremendous amount of earned media through their celebration.

- The way the company reveals new products and concocts presale madness, like the live stream unveiling of their groundbreaking Cyber Truck

- The way Elon Musk personally responds and posts social content to keep people updated, entertained, and in awe

- The way that Tesla builds excitement, announcing advancements like the first of its kind Giga-Press, which Tesla says will revolutionize car production

- The way Tesla builds excitement and influence from their associations with SpaceX and The Boring Company

- The way customers create content, like fully produced commercials, dedicated YouTube Channels, or gleaming social posts and reviews
- The way Tesla team members film educational videos, like the YouTube post during COVID-19 that provided an engineering update on the Tesla Ventilator being developed from car parts
- The way A-list Tesla owners like Matt Damon, Leonardo DiCaprio, Cameron Diaz, and Katy Perry enthusiastically support Tesla and create an avalanche of influence ... free of charge

These are only a few of the ways that Tesla sustains an aura of inspiration and participation that surrounds the brand. Their comprehensive brand story celebration is an excellent example of how Culture Development Marketing keeps your brand relevant, impactful, and evolving.

REMEMBER: YOUR COMPANY HAS TO KEEP ITS PROMISES.

Celebrating your story is a team sport. The more players on your team, the better. But how do you forge brand celebrators? You have to share your story in a way that inspires energy, enthusiasm, and support.

Delivering on your promises is critical, and everyone inside the brand **needs** to recognize and respect that responsibility. The value and importance of the brand story ought to be spread throughout the organization. Your people must be compelled to engage with your brand: it should be authentic and enticing. It has to call like-minded people to the inside.

Make sure that people inside and outside your brand are able to:

- Relate to your brand's Attitude
- Understand your brand's Drive

- Gain confidence in your brand's Direction

Attitude, Drive, and Direction are the three components of a comprehensive story—the building blocks that open up the opportunities for brand story involvement, integration, and participation. Communicate these areas effectively and they will validate the story and secure trust.

TRUST IS THE THREAD THAT KNITS YOUR COMPANY AND YOUR STORY TOGETHER

Each area appeals to a person in different ways, although all are critical factors in building trust, and therefore the most important components of your story. Culture Development Marketing cannot take place without trust. In fact, every principle, action, and idea associated with the process of CDM is fueled and built by the currency gained through trust.

———

YOU CANNOT BUILD OR ESTABLISH ANYTHING LONG-TERM THROUGH YOUR BRAND STORY IF PEOPLE DON'T TRUST AND BELIEVE IN IT.

———

For that reason, your defined brand story must build trust in a comprehensive way: The message and meaning need to be complete. It has to meet the needs of all personality types. It is essential to realize that people have different triggers to spark, inspire, and validate trust. Everyone is wired differently:

- The emotional side of the brand moves some people
- The way a brand operates stimulates other people
- The brand's results and reputation provide confidence to others

A brand story that includes the Attitude, Drive, and Direction of the brand covers all these bases. Defining these three elements validates trust on every level by connecting comprehensively.

Trust validation breaks down barriers by opening up the opportunity to connect, influence, and inspire. You won't ensure success without it.

NO FAKE FRIENDS, NO FAKE BRANDS

The public doesn't want "phony" people in their lives. For the same reasons, folks don't like fake brands or fake stories. Consumers have too many options. They can't waste their time and effort by attaching themselves to brands they don't believe in.

When searching for an authentic attachment, people need to believe in the story. To do that, it's essential that they connect with it in a way that allows them to build trust and confidence. However, individuals develop trust in their own way. When brands tell one-dimensional stories, they wind up unnecessarily missing the mark with many potential celebrators because they fail to include essential aspects of the narrative.

When you tell a **complete** story—engaging the emotional and operational sides of the story, and those who seek results—you give eager people what they need to bond and build trust in your brand. You check all the boxes, providing enough context to produce trust by connecting in a compelling and engaging way.

Let's take a closer look at how each of these story components aids the story by validating trust.

3 WAYS YOUR STORY CAN
— VALIDATE TRUST —

EMOTIONAL VALIDATION

These are your "LISTEN TO YOUR HEART" people

They prefer to establish trust through a
personal connection they can feel.

They are looking to connect with the brand's
passion, emotion, and energy.

OPERATIONAL VALIDATION

These are your "TRUST THE PROCESS" people

They prefer to establish trust through a detailed
understanding of the brand's functionality.

They are looking to examine the systems,
processes, strategies, and tools that allow the
brand to successfully function and operate.

EMPIRICAL VALIDATION

These are your "SEE IT TO BELIEVE IT" people

They prefer to establish trust through
verifiable observations and experiences,
rather than theory or pure logic.

They are looking to gain a clear picture of
where the experience is going by examining
information that validates the brand's
performance, reputation, and results.

EMOTIONAL PEOPLE: "I WANT TO FEEL GOOD ABOUT IT"

A brand story must connect on an emotional level. Appealing to the emotions provides a vehicle that will fast-track trust-building. Emotional storytelling caters to the people who have a need to understand the attitude of the brand to develop a deeper relationship and bond.

Science supports the importance and impact of this connection. Neuroeconomist Paul Zak discovered an important connection between oxytocin and stories. Oxytocin is a hormone that plays an important role in fostering trust and connection. It's called the "love hormone" for the way it releases in the body when we feel trust, when we are the object of kindness, or when we make a connection with someone.

Zak found that oxytocin also releases when we listen to stories that we connect with emotionally. The presence of oxytocin encourages a higher level of trust. As a result, the story not only allows us to feel differently through the emotions we experience, but it also strengthens the connection to the story because oxytocin is also increasing the level of trust.

Whether or not you believe the science, emotional validation is essential to your brand because, for many people, it is priority number one. It's common sense to understand that every strong relationship involves some type of emotional attachment. If you want to set your brand story up to build trust and long-term relationships, you need to generate emotion.

That doesn't mean every brand story has to evoke intense feelings of love in order to validate trust. It simply means that whether the personality of your brand is personal or impersonal, you need to clarify and convey the way emotion exists in it so people can recognize it and relate to your personality. Simply focus on defining your attitude and then celebrating it as part of your story in a clear and consistent manner.

OPERATIONAL PEOPLE: "HOW WILL THAT WORK?"

Operational storytelling celebrates the distinctive actions and processes that drive your brand's success. This type of messaging influences consumers who want to "trust the process." Operational evaluation and appreciation builds their trust, and the educational content encourages assurance and belief in the way things are getting done. Such people gain confidence through the understanding of the inner workings of the brand.

Shining a light on these specialized areas communicates differentiating value in the way the brand functions and operates. By presenting unique ways in which the brand works, people can understand how the brand performs and functions, often giving them insight on how they can take part in the story.

EMPIRICAL PEOPLE: "NO MORE BULLSHIT; GIVE ME THE FACTS"

Some people need data and facts to connect—as we all do, to a degree. Somewhere inside the brain is a part that is tired of listening to bullshit. It has simply had enough and doesn't want to listen to theories, hypotheses, or assumptions any longer. For some people, this brain component may be the largest part, and for others, it may only represent a tiny factor. But at some level, everyone values empirical validation because we all realize that talk is cheap.

Empirical validation isn't about solidifying an end result to the experience; it is an open-ended, continual authentication of the experience. Empirical storytelling evolves through the constant presence of provable statements and measured outcomes—hard evidence of performance that validates the story and backs up the brand's promises.

Empirical support connects with outcome-oriented consumers who need verified information to gain trust and connection. Put simply, these people want to understand the brand's path and its promise. They respond to the presence of empirical proof, documentation, and data in your brand story.

CULTURE DEVELOPMENT MARKETING SUMMARY

CDM is centered around creating a celebration that consistently educates on these three story components to validate trust on all levels. It is an ongoing process that sets your company up to stand out, to make progress continually, and to evolve. The process is not for everyone because the idea of defining your story, creating a plan to celebrate that story, and then working together to execute a story celebration plan is a commitment that some company leaders may not want to make. For that reason, many stories never get celebrated.

THE EASY ROAD TO NOWHERE

The Tell-to-Sell method is quicker and less involved than a Celebrate-to-Educate approach. It requires less commitment and setup, and conversions come quicker. You can easily craft a story to get conversions and sales, and it doesn't even have to be accurate or authentic. However, if something is easy but it doesn't work, is there really any value to it? The problem with taking the easy road to brand story development is that the message dead-ends and becomes muffled as consumers grow tired of hearing the same stories. They tune out what you say, so it becomes more difficult for brands to gain any attention at all—and the problem is only getting worse.

The process of CDM is about setting up a celebration around a story that doesn't dead-end. When you commit to this path, it elevates your brand, allowing you to stand out and build long-term relationships. You set your brand up for continued success because the brand and message evolve through celebration and participation. The story doesn't stop.

ATTITUDE, DRIVE, AND DIRECTION EVOLUTION

The components of Attitude, Drive, and Direction don't just build trust in the brand story. They create connection points that allow the brand to grow and develop. We are all drawn to aspects of each of these components.

Continuously presenting related examples and illustrations will help each area advance through new interest, ideas, and innovation. It is important to understand how each of these areas can develop. This awareness will help you as you evaluate the relevancy of your story and storylines annually. When conditions shift, you may adjust the story and storylines to meet the needs of your company.

ATTITUDE SHAPES PERSONALITY

Brand attitude is the constant of the three story elements: Attitude, Drive, and Direction. Although a consumer can have varying opinions from day to day, consistent brand attitudes are vital. Defining that Attitude lets you understand the range in which your brand personality can shift authentically.

Understanding the scope of your brand's attitude provides flexibility that can help a brand decide which content, ideas, and actions are aligned and which are not. It also enables you to find the best ways to relate and empathize when needed. Each of these benefits increases your ability to connect and resonate with potential brand celebrators.

DRIVE EARNS RESPECT

Brand drive celebrations reinforce the habits, systems, routines, and standards that move your brand forward. These are foundational actions and ideas that define the brand. Ideally, it would be great if these brand story behaviors remained consistent. However, factors like the economy, technology, competition, and many others can effect change in this area. Opening up the opportunity to receive input will allow you to continually build and develop the functionality and performance of your brand.

Drive is about the way you do things—how you operate. In the 1980s, the NBA flourished with the famous battles between Larry Bird's "blue-collar" Boston Celtics teams versus Magic Johnson's "showtime" LA Lakers. Both teams operated in the opposite way: the Lakers played with speed and finesse, and the Celtics thrived on fierce defense. They had opposite styles, but both had respect for one another.

DIRECTION ILLUSTRATES WHERE THE EXPERIENCE WILL TAKE YOU

Every brand has expectations. If you went into a Gordon Ramsay restaurant and got a McDonald's burger, you'd be more irate than Gordon in his latest episode of *Hell's Kitchen*. Conversely, if you went to McDonald's and the process took two hours and cost $400, you probably wouldn't be Lovin' It.

The Direction of the brand evolves as real-world developments and brand experiences are understood and reflected back by participants. The proof of empirical support keeps the message moving, verifying the ideas and experiences associated with the story. Provable facts and results can help build trust, but their impact isn't eternal and must be continually verified. A brand story celebration that supplies an ongoing flow of verifiable content is important in helping to boost trust and confidence, while also keeping naysayers at bay.

The CDM process allows the story to live on through the celebration of your Attitude, Drive, and Direction. Examples and illustrations continue to help the story evolve: you keep on educating, you keep on connecting with people, and you keep on inspiring participation.

ATTITUDE, DRIVE, AND DIRECTION REINFORCE EACH OTHER

Clearly defining these components affords everyone surrounding the brand with the ability to visualize success, connect with the meaning, and establish trust in the brand on their own terms. This transformational magic happens when you detail your Attitude, Drive, and Direction in combination. Grouping them together and then defining them allows them to become greater. Each area transitions into a more deliberate and intentional form that clarifies the brand's inspiring aspects.

Uncovering your brand story is like a chemistry experiment because it involves compounding ingredients to design the desired effect. Attitude, Drive, and Direction are the ingredients, and the desired result of the experiment is to reveal a core story. The process requires you to explore, understand, and detail each of these areas. Defining them together stimulates a chain reaction of connection: they borrow from each other to become more than they are apart.

As you uncover your company's most inspiring aspects in each of these areas, the brand structure and storylines emerge. The process of uncovering your brand story to define your Attitude, Drive, and Direction is amazing. There is a magical interdependence between the three components, and when you merge them into a comprehensive story, you create a state of peak performance called the **3-P Principle**®.

SUMMARY:

- Build a party, not a lecture.
- A brand celebration needs people who are interested, excited, and integrated with your brand.
- Identify the real things that matter and make a plan to elevate them in a way that allows you to attract similar people who are also interested in them.

CHAPTER SIX

Positive, Powerful, Purposeful: The 3-P Principle®

ANY TIMES, THE whole is greater than the sum of its parts. Bacon is amazing, eggs are incredible, and toast can be awesome. However, when you combine them together, you tap into a secret synergy that allows the flavors from each ingredient to intensify. The chemistry between bacon, eggs, and toast cannot be denied as they combine to construct the perfect breakfast.

This type of harmonious combination exists in story development. A few key ingredients together transform the narrative to become something greater. You combine a clearly defined Attitude, Drive, and Direction, and magic happens.

Your Attitude shifts to **Positive**, your Drive becomes **Powerful**, and your Direction becomes **Purposeful**. Together, they are much greater than their individual component ingredients. This is the 3-P Principle®.

Building a story in this comprehensive way allows you to connect with your message, resonate on a personal level, and inspire individuals to participate in your brand story celebration. The combination will unlock the ability to build trust with your message because it is real and authentic on every level.

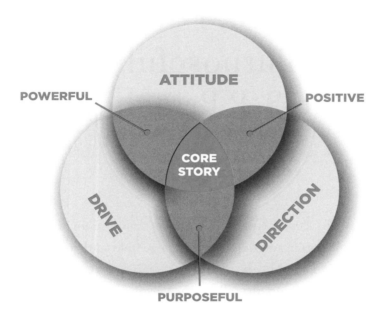

Countless business and leadership books have been written on all three of these components. Each is a critically important area, and defining them in isolation will undoubtedly help you achieve some clarity. However, when you define and combine these aspects simultaneously, the alliance enables each area to evolve into something more.

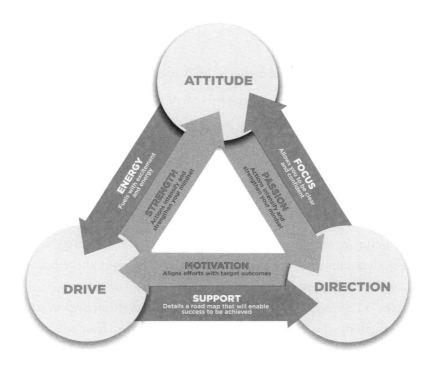

YOUR ATTITUDE

- Receives confidence and Focus from your Direction
- Your Attitude borrows intensity and Strength from your Drive
- Elevates to become POSITIVE

YOUR DRIVE

- Becomes inspired through the Energy of your Attitude
- Adds Motivation through clear goals and Direction
- Solidifies to become POWERFUL

YOUR DIRECTION

- Becomes dedicated through the Support of your Drive
- Gets personal through the Passion of your Attitude
- Clarifies to become PURPOSEFUL

These descriptions outline the interdependency of the 3-P Principle®, illustrating how each area transforms when grouped and defined. The amazing exchange occurs in each relationship as the components borrow strength from one another and the most inspiring aspects of your brand merge into a clear and concise brand story summary. Don't make your summary wordy or dense. Keep it relevant and relatable, saying less and influencing more.

The 3-P Principle® makes a tremendous impact on an organization by unearthing a perspective that allows the brand to increase education, elevate understanding, and build trust on every level. This type of connection changes the game by shifting the brand into focus. It clarifies a comprehensive story, makes it easy to pinpoint ideal storylines, and sets the brand up for long-term success.

Let's take a look at a company that was able to change the trajectory of their business through the 3-P Principle.®

—

CHANGE YOUR WATER.
CHANGE YOUR LIFE.

—

In 2017, my wife's dermatologist suggested that our home's tap water could be a contributing factor to her ongoing issues with psoriasis. Researching the issue, I found that chlorine and contaminants were a common problem in Southwest Florida. A plumbing company tested the water and it confirmed that our tap water had high chlorine levels and other harmful ingredients.

The plumbing company suggested a HALO 5 whole-home water filtration system, which was installed a few days later. I wasn't sure exactly how it worked, but the silver cylinder looked magnificent. It didn't take long for me to learn that the system delivers. The results were amazing.

The HALO 5 made my water taste insanely fresh, it helped my wife's skin issues disappear, and it stopped our fixtures from deteriorating. Beyond impressed, I loved the system so much that I wanted to learn more about the company. I clicked over to the HALO Water Systems website, and I was quickly confused. The HALO 5 filter installed in my home was sleek, cool, and innovative. But their website was dated, bland, and underwhelming. There I was, ready to learn more to start celebrating, but there was no story to start the party. I saw an opportunity.

I did some digging and learned that HALO is a national water filtration company that has been successfully operating for over two decades. I easily saw that the company suffered from a fragmented story. Their marketing was clearly failing to provide education on their most inspiring aspects.

I contacted HALO's founder and CEO, Glen Blavet, and he was in full agreement that their story wasn't being translated. He agreed to go through the process of CDM.

Here's how that process helped HALO define their story's core components:

- **HALO's Defined Attitude:** HALO's foundation is built from their founder's passionate belief that water quality is critically important for everyone. His love and appreciation for water quality started when he became a plumber, it intensified as he became a contractor, and it began to change lives when he created HALO Water Systems. This contagious passion allowed the HALO team to wholeheartedly adopt the belief that water quality should be fun, easy, and essential.

- **HALO's Defined Drive:** HALO's unparalleled quality standards are directly related to the core commitment they have to plumbing contractors. Every HALO solution is specifically designed to be contractor-grade. In fact, HALO products are intentionally created "For the contractor, by a contractor." In addition, every HALO system and solution has been designed to help educate people on all reasons that people "Gotta have a HALO." The goal is to make it easy for plumbers to educate homeowners on all the ways that HALO water quality solutions can change their lives.

- **HALO's Defined Direction:** The fact that HALO was established by a contractor for contractors also plays a role in the company's target outcomes. Their goal is to create solutions that enable plumbers to deliver upon a promise to "protect the health and safety of the nation." HALO water quality solutions make it easy for plumbing contractors to change the lives of their customers by providing them with solutions that enable them to have clean, healthy water throughout the home.

Let's take a look at HALO's resulting Brand Story Summary.

We discussed how the 3-P Principle® transitions key components of a brand story into something greater. Now let's examine how it worked with HALO. The breakdown below illustrates how defining each of these areas allows them to gain strength from each other.

HOW THE 3-P PRINCIPLE® BROUGHT OUT THE BEST IN HALO WATER

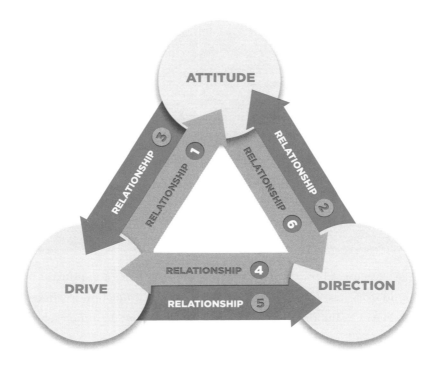

Relationship 1 | HALO's Attitude is strengthened by a Defined Drive:

HALO's attitude is reinforced by clear quality standards and aligned systems. The union makes their passion actionable and understood.

- When you identify the habits, systems, and processes that drive success, your attitude feeds off the confidence. When actions strengthen attitude, the integration forms an intentional mindset.

Relationship 2 | **HALO's Attitude gains focus from a Defined Direction:**

Clear outcomes allow HALO to become focused and intentional.

- HALO's company was built from the founder's passion for good water quality. This connection makes HALO's partnership with contractors unique. HALO's focus on education makes the company-wide goal of changing lives through water quality more understandable, relatable, and meaningful.

Relationship 3 | **HALO's Drive gains energy from their Defined Attitude:**

HALO's passionate attitude adds fuel to their systems and actions.

- Once the founder's passion was identified, the actions, systems, and standards could be executed with emotion. If you want to grow your brand, your attitude and energy cannot be a secret. They have to be transferable.

Relationship 4 | **HALO's Drive receives motivation from their Defined Direction:**

HALO supercharges their processes by connecting them to their purpose.

- A defined outcome aligns your actions to a recognized outcome. Visualizing the finish line increases your power and production immensely by allowing you to run with certainty.

Relationship 5 | **HALO's Direction gains passion from their Defined Attitude:**

HALO's team morale gains inspiration, and their work became more meaningful.

- Combine a Defined Attitude with a clear vision of the outcomes you aim to accomplish, and you gain the courage and commitment you need to be successful. Your objectives become inspired, and you inject passion into your desired outcomes.

Relationship 6 | **HALO's Direction receives support from their Defined Drive:**

HALO understands what they are doing, why they are doing it, and what they are working toward.

- HALO was able to connect the dots to clarify how their commitment to contractor training makes it easy to relay knowledge to plumbers, who pass this education on to the homeowner. It's a purposeful domino effect that everyone in the company plays a role in.

Uncovering the HALO story outlined single definitions for their Attitude, Drive, and Direction. However, the real progress occurred through the resulting clarity that allowed each component to work together, unlocking potential that was previously unrecognized or undervalued.

—

RESULTS THAT ARE
POSITIVE, POWERFUL, AND PURPOSEFUL®

—

Alignment is a monstrous payoff that the 3-P Principle® provides. It helps solidify your culture, powers your processes, and enables you to influence on a whole new level. For example, the process of uncovering HALO's story led to a brand story celebration that sparked a steady and substantial increase in distribution and sales. HALO secured partnerships in dozens of extra markets, increasing sales 30 percent in 2019, 35 percent in 2020, and projecting to double their business in 2021. It's been an amazing turnaround.

In fact, HALO's CEO and founder Glen Blavet proudly points out the irony in HALO's newly defined brand story title: "Change Your Water. Change Your Life." He states that his decision to implement Culture Development Marketing and

> To see HALO founder Glen Blavet talk about the impact of CDM in his own words, go to EveryoneIsAnInfluencer.com/Halo.

start celebrating HALO's story "changed my company and my life." It's a powerful testimony for the impact of the 3-P Principle.®

THE 3-P PRINCIPLE® CONNECTS INFLUENCERS AT EVERY LEVEL

The framework of the 3-P Principle® sets up the creation of a story that builds trust on all levels. Keep in mind that "all levels" never means "all people." No message will hit home with everyone who comes into contact with it, nor does it need to. The most popular television shows in America make billions for their networks by only capturing 2–3 percent of the viewing audience. When you focus on similar people, you'll gain support ... and results you'll love.

The goal is to reach the right people with the right message. Seek to onboard truly enthusiastic people who are a right fit with your brand: the influencers who matter most.

These ideal influencers are the customers, friends, and followers who get what you do. Different backgrounds, perspectives, and experiences allow them to bond with your story uniquely.

Remember, people connect in different ways: with emotions, with operations, and with empirical results.

Emotional connectors primarily feel trust instinctively through the personality of the brand, so they can have a comfortable relationship with it. They look for a positive attitude.

Operational connectors are more practical and want to review your processes and systems to visualize the brand experience in action. They build trust through understanding the way your brand functions in a reliable, dependable fashion. They are impressed with a powerful drive.

Results-oriented connectors primarily care about what your company does, and want proof of performance to build trust through the facts and the details that educate them about the outcome of their experience. They want to see a purposeful direction.

The best brands in the world communicate trust in each of these areas by celebrating a comprehensive story:

- They want people to feel something emotionally.
- They are transparent and display how they operate.
- They are courageous enough to illustrate the results they deliver and the changes they have made and continue to make.

Team members, customers, and other like-minded people bond with stories that include all three elements because they want to feel the feeling, understand the actions, and be part of the change. You have to make it easy for individuals to join in the celebration—connecting, understanding, and appreciating your story on every level.

GOING BEYOND TRANSACTIONAL TARGETING

Today, branding involves tagging, targeting, and retargeting to create conversions at lightning speed, taking customers down a quick funnel to convert them into a sale. The idea is quick gains and smart sales, but it's not a relationship-building process. Quick conversion tactics should definitely play a prominent role in your marketing plan, but not take the lead in your brand story celebration.

A big difference exists between selling people and building relationships. Evolving technology has an amazing ability to target demographics and psychographics in marketing, and Telling-and-Selling is often automated. But automation is impersonal. For your brand to connect in a way that moves people to become influencers who celebrate your story, you have to educate them on a comprehensive story.

When any one of the core components is absent from the brand's story, the story loses strength and power. The ideas cannot fully integrate together, and instead of a tight-knit, solid story, the narrative is disorganized and unclear.

A clearly defined, comprehensive story brings the core components together to form a Positive mentality, a Powerful mindset, and a Purposeful vision. This focus sets you up for success by simplifying content creation. It reveals storylines that allow you to outline a game plan for education, growth, and forward progress.

Using the 3-P Principle® results in this type of connection. It generates a story that can be visualized, understood, and believed, and provides the type of clarity that multiplies your chances for progress and success in brand development, in business, and in life.

STORYLINES OPEN 3-P® CONNECTION OPPORTUNITIES

One of the main benefits of the 3-P Principle® is the way it simplifies content creation. It's easy to see which insights and ideas are aligned with the story and should be celebrated. Once a comprehensive brand story summary exists, your goal is to create a celebration that educates people about the story, which acts as a barometer to gauge what content ideas make sense. You make this process easier by extending the message of the brand story summary through storylines that highlight story aspects, ideas, or initiatives.

Your summary is the core story, and your storylines are extensions that reach out and allow connections to be made in different ways. Each storyline spells out specific promises, ideas, and expectations associated with brand performance. Storylines form a shared avenue for story education and expression, where coordinated ideas travel into and out from the brand.

Coordinating content in this manner provides a simple road map for identifying celebration-worthy content. The rule is ...

—

ATTITUDE IS THE EMOTION THAT THE BRAND CARRIES.

DRIVE REPRESENTS HOW THE BRAND OPERATES.

DIRECTION DETAILS WHERE THE
BRAND EXPERIENCE WILL LEAD.

—

This rule is vital in the goal of educating on the story, building value, and being inspiring with no more guesswork. This structure directs focus to executing the ideas and actions with the most robust connection and highest value. Content creation isn't about games or manipulating the truth. Instead, seize the opportunity to lead the conversation by educating others about the personality, values, and promises that you KNOW you can back up.

THE 3 P'S BRING EVERYTHING INTO FOCUS

Is all this promotion needed if the brand already possesses these characteristics? The brand narrative may already be present and is seen through the eyes of the customer or team member. However, when a brand decides to isolate these ideas and showcase them, the celebration magnifies their presence and makes them clear to see, consistently recognized, and increasingly present. This illustrates the depth and authenticity of your brand story while accentuating that your story isn't just hype. The more you do this, the more you solidify confidence and drive value.

A brand story celebration is an ongoing commitment for constant improvement through listening, learning, and growing. When the public understands this commitment, their loyalty and appreciation increases and the story doesn't dead-end or disappoint, remaining real and relatable, and supporters are inspired to add to it. Build trust in the journey and the story will continue to take shape and evolve every day.

—

THE 3-P PRINCIPLE® HELPS YOUR PEOPLE
UNDERSTAND A MEANINGFUL CULTURE.

—

Defining who you are as a brand is nothing new. It has long been common practice for committees and key decision makers to explore values, discuss the vision, and consider target markets. Often, brand leaders are tasked with deciding what the brand is all about. They instill their own beliefs, coordinate their thoughts into succinct words to organize a set of core values, or define a company mission or vision statement. These instruments are valuable, but they are different from creating a brand story summary through the process of CDM.

This difference is that CDM establishes a brand story summary through a process of uncovering. It has not been created by management, and it has not been invented by a marketing team. If you want to inspire an army of influencers to celebrate your story, build your brand story from perceptions the brand has already earned.

> If you want to inspire an army of influencers to celebrate your story, build your brand story from perceptions the brand has already earned.

An authentic brand story isn't about aspirations, and it isn't an approach centered on an experience you hope to induce. CDM is about uncovering today's reputation and learning who you are on a relatable level. These understandings will then shine a light on your most inspiring aspects, allowing you to do more of what makes you successful.

An authentic brand story needs to be human and relatable so team members and leaders can see themselves in it and understand the importance of their role in the story. That's why the process of CDM is intentionally driven by individuals.

Many times, the mission statements, goals, and value propositions were written at a level above everyone's head and represent a vision of what the brand aspires to be. When the message isn't based on who you are right now, team members, customers, and clients will all have a hard time connecting with and believing your story. The dating profile won't match up, and the relationship is almost automatically poisoned by a lack of trust and disappointment.

—

FIND YOUR VALUES. DON'T INVENT THEM.

—

Living an authentic brand story should come naturally. I've seen many organizations train their team to memorize corporate mission statements so they can't repeat the words back on demand. I've never been a fan of this strategy. Gaining brand story appreciation should be based on each individual's authentic interpretation of the story. People don't need to repeat your story or mission statement like members of a cult, your culture isn't a dictatorship.

Instead of telling people your story, show them—and make it easy for them to be a part of it. The objective is to lead others to recognize, value, and be inspired by the brand's story, developing their confidence to participate on their own terms. When you mandate your brand storytelling in a specific way, you miss the input, energy, and ideas that participation brings. It also takes away a like-minded person's ability to personalize their version of the story.

Open up the narrative through a brand story celebration and people are able to see themselves as part of a bigger story, instinctively understanding what they can contribute. Telling your story is a non-inclusive sharing style that gets the point across but contains no invitation for involvement. Celebrating your story plugs people in. Feeling part of a larger vision also taps into the human quest for meaning and purpose— the need to make an impact.

DNA AND YOUR BRAND

Think of your organization as a body, and imagine the people who make it up as single cells. Just like in a body, cells need a blueprint to understand how they function successfully as part of the whole—they need DNA. Your core brand story acts as your company's DNA. This story supplies your business's "rules" behind all its interactions and processes. It is already there in the cells of the body. You don't add it, it unfolds.

Like DNA, the story is the blueprint of what follows: one little set of instructions on 26 chromosomes provide for the massive amounts of genetic diversity in the human species.

Before the internet upped the game on accountability, the idea was to invent the story you wanted to tell. You can still do that—have your best team of thought leaders concoct a touching brand story that makes heads nod around that conference table. However, if the touchpoints of the brand can't be consistently reinforced with appropriate behaviors and actions, the story is ultimately fiction. If you claim to have integrity but deliberately cut corners, the story you are selling makes the situation worse. You won't create or sustain support for long, and your brand celebration will be a flash in the pan.

Understanding the 3-P Principle® enables you to connect in a greater way, but you have to put in work to make this principle possible. With that in mind, in the next chapter we will outline the steps you'll take to gain the awareness and understanding needed to benefit from the 3-P Principle.® Culture Development Marketing provides this perspective because it is conducted through the steps of revealing, assessing, combining, and elevating. This R.A.C.E. process is how you unlock the power of the 3-P Principle® and set your company up for long-term success in celebrating its story.

SUMMARY:

- People connect in different ways: with emotions, with operations, and with empirical results.

- The 3-P Principle® sets up the creation of a story that increases education, elevates understanding, and builds trust on every level.

- If you want to inspire an army of influencers to celebrate your story, build your brand story from perceptions the brand has already earned.

- The R.A.C.E. process creates an understanding that makes the 3-P Principle® possible.

CHAPTER SEVEN

Finding the Way to What's Real and True: A Foundation That Multiplies Your Efforts

REMEMBER WHO YOU are. *The Lion King* is a classic tale. Simba is a young lion set to inherit the kingdom from his father. In a moment of selfishness and rebellion, Simba is chased away from his pride, and then his evil uncle Scar murders his father to take the throne for himself. Simba spends time away from home, but eventually learns that his lands are barren because his uncle is unfit to be king. Scar has mismanaged everything.

Simba is unsure of what to do. However, his fear, doubt, and uncertainty go away when he hears his father's voice say, "Remember who you are." This moment of enlightenment connects him with his father's spirit of justice and goodness, helping him find the bravery to win back the kingdom he was born to lead. Simba transforms as well: from a spoiled child to the leader his kingdom desperately needs.

When you know who you are, you gain clarity, confidence, and the ability to bridge and integrate new ideas into your culture while protecting your earned reputation. Keep in mind that you have to preserve your story and live up to what it promises through every aspect of innovation and development.

—

VALUE THE BRAND STORY EXPERIENCE YOU DELIVER,
APPRECIATE WHO YOU TRULY ARE,
AND MAKE MOVES WITH THAT MINDSET.

—

THE CORE COMPONENTS OF CULTURE DEVELOPMENT MARKETING

The process of CDM helps you understand who you are and how your company is being perceived by isolating the ways you deliver value.

I spent over a decade formalizing the process of CDM into a series of steps in a repeatable format. Since then, I have spent another decade using this operation exclusively with my team and clients. The formalized steps to execute the process are built around an easy-to-remember R.A.C.E. acronym. The goal is to give you clarity in understanding the mechanism at the granular level: Reveal, Assess, Combine, and Elevate.

- It begins with mapping perception patterns.
- It grows through understanding how these impressions are being earned.
- It comes together through story summarization.
- It flourishes through the celebration of that story.

Let's take a look at an outline of how you can R.A.C.E. through this four-step CDM process:

- **Reveal** the story by extracting and understanding the ideas that matter most through an Impression Analysis.

- **Assess** the story by executing a brand story survey that will allow you to clarify how the results of the Impression Analysis have been earned.

- **Combine** the connection points into a comprehensive brand story summary.

- **Elevate** the most inspiring aspects of your brand through the celebration of your brand's story.

START AT THE END

The details matter. The process of CDM consists of uncovering your brand story, working the information down from its broadest perspective to its tightest definition. The process works in reverse when thinking of how you experience the story as a reader.

When you uncover a story as a reader ...

- The title grabs your attention

- Then you preview the story summary to see if you connect with it

- You read what happens to understand how the story unfolds

- And you finish the book to come away with an impression

In contrast, the steps to follow to uncover a story work in reverse. Here is how using the process of CDM works:

- First review the resulting impressions to gain awareness of the associated story outcomes.

- Then dig in to learn how the story is developed, and to clarify how these impressions are being earned.

- Combine the findings into a brand story summary that conveys the meaning of the story.

- Finally, conceive a title that captures the essence and energy of the story in a simple, relatable brand message.

KEEPING PACE HAS A PAYOFF

The R.A.C.E. to uncover your brand story through CDM happens one layer at a time. In reviewing each layer, we won't move too fast or go too far in the wrong direction. The pace should allow all readers to stay together.

You may be the CEO or business owner, hoping this isn't going to turn into a tactical marketing workbook. Or you may be wondering why a breakdown of the execution ideas is relevant to you. Your time is valuable, and to benefit from this book, only the relevant knowledge, ideas, and insight are included to allow you to understand and appreciate the process.

The brand leaders who actually manage and execute the process will be given a basic description of the tools, an explanation of how to execute them, and some tools to download online. However, to keep this book focused on leadership, I will spare you the deep procedure talk and do my best to give you what you need to know.

In providing a high-level overview, this book delivers the ability to recognize the reasoning and rationale behind the process, along with the clarity to decide if CDM is a fit for you.

Everyone Is An Influencer is the title because this mindset is centered on an understanding and appreciation of how celebrating your story can change everything for your organization. This valuable mentality supplies you with the ability to inspire everyone involved with your company to have more fun and success. That's not a bad deliverable.

The rest of this chapter will explore the insight and ideas needed to gain the right perspective for beginning the R.A.C.E.: the importance of being who you are, taking into account the value you deliver, and confidently embracing your own story, regardless of the challenges and competition. However, before we further discuss the steps of the R.A.C.E., let's review a lesson from an actual race that would have been amazing to see.

—

CHAMPIONS ARE NOT CREATED EQUAL.

—

Englishman Roger Bannister ran track in the 1950s and is considered by many to be one of the most revolutionary runners of all time. Michael Johnson is an Olympic champion from the United States who raced in the 1990s, and is also considered to be one of the greatest runners ever to set foot on a track.

Imagine being able to transport both of these incredible athletes, at the peak of their prime, to the same track to compete in an epic race. The event will be a single lap around the track, which everyone is excited to witness. Bannister and Johnson are stretching, getting ready, and as the race draws near, the two competitors move to the starting line. The crowd rises to their feet, roaring in anticipation.

The two champions position themselves in the starting blocks. Roger seems a bit uncomfortable, while Michael appears steel-faced and focused. The time has come for this blockbuster matchup, and the starting gun fires.

Wow. Immediately you notice Johnson bursting out of the starting blocks, jumping ahead from the start. He continues to accelerate and widen his lead. As Johnson powers through the finish line, it is apparent that he has left Bannister in the dust, crushing the Englishman.

After a long debate, it is decided that something must have gone wrong. The two champions agree to come back to the blocks and run the race again. The outcome is identical. In fact, they run the race ten more times and Johnson wins every time. The outcome is never even close.

How could this happen? Two of the best to ever run a race and they are running at the fastest pace of their career, but it's not competitive?

It happens because the race didn't match up with Bannister's talents and abilities. He was a middle-distance runner who famously became the first person to run a mile in under four minutes. In contrast, Johnson was a sprinter who won four Olympic gold medals and held the World and Olympic records in the 200 meter and 400 meter events. Regardless of how many times these two ran a 400 meter race, Bannister would never win. But if you put them both on a track and had them run a mile, then Johnson's quickness would eventually succumb to Bannister's endurance, and Bannister would win the race.

—

IT'S THE SAME IN BUSINESS. IT SEEMS LIKE EVERYONE IS RUNNING THE SAME RACE, REGARDLESS OF WHETHER THE RACE IS RIGHT FOR THEM OR NOT.

—

Companies don't want to miss out on competing in any aspect, so businesses say the same things in the same way and try to win the same customers. They recruit team members with identical benefits. They claim to deliver the same outcomes. They blend together more than ever, and the cluttered field constitutes an unwinnable race.

—

YOU CAN'T BLEND IN AND STILL WIN.

—

When your company blends in, it becomes predictable and easily beaten—someone is always faster or cheaper. However, when you focus on running a race that lines up with your talents and abilities, you can outdistance your competition and separate yourself from the pack by doing more, being more, and going further.

If the race doesn't suit you, you'll spend too much time worrying about how well you match up against others. Instead, concentrate on being the best you can be and make other people run YOUR race, where you have all the advantages and all the cards.

Your organization may possess world-class attributes that can be used to position your brand to be distinct and dominate the competition. But if the focus isn't on leading your efforts through the celebration of these most inspiring attributes, you won't achieve long-term success. When you fail to clarify and celebrate your story, your brand becomes misunderstood and undervalued ... and you blend in with everyone else.

Blending in puts you in the uncomfortable position of being obsessed with competitor comparisons. Many companies go wrong when they spend far too much time matching offers, creating rebuttal campaigns, and plotting how they can beat other companies at their own game. And they inevitably have to lower their prices (and margins), putting their business at risk.

Reactionary strategies can be an essential slice of your marketing, but they should never define you. When your business is structured and designed to match up with others, you will eventually compete in an area that is unsuitable for you. You not only miss out on the opportunity to connect with the individuals who matter most, but you also set your brand up to be assessed and valued

> When your business is structured and designed to match up with others, you will eventually compete in an area that is unsuitable for you.

on terms that aren't aligned with your talents and abilities. Brands that do this find it difficult to compete. They end up being left in the dust like Roger Bannister, trying to win a race he wasn't built for.

WHAT TO DO WHEN CHANGE HAPPENS

Sometimes the market changes and a business is forced to adjust the race it's running. These developments can sneak up on any company and pressure them to make decisions to protect their future. Yes, when it comes to brand story development, some of the worst shit happens when shift happens.

Multinational coffee/donut company Dunkin' knows a lot about brand shifting. The business started in 1950 and has changed a lot over the years through numerous buyouts, acquisitions, and other brand-related changes. Recently, they created a buzz when they dropped the "Donuts" out of their brand image, changing their name from Dunkin' Donuts to Dunkin' in early 2019.

This iconic brand's name change is the latest in a series of maneuvers they've made in the last decade to evolve the brand into a beverage-led, on-the-go business. Change has been a way of life for the Dunkin' brand. Their industry changes so much and so fast that continual shifting is mandatory. However, change isn't easy.

In 1997, Dunkin' Donuts chose to end their award-winning "Time to Make the Donuts!" campaign. The company realized that its brand would need a healthier identity for the future, but they struggled to find a solution. In 2004, their "America Runs on Dunkin'" campaign methodically redefined the company as a beverage-led, on-the-go brand. The longtime donut dealer found a creative way to attach health, energy, and vibrancy attributes into their story by associating them with their flagship, blue-collar coffee. It was a stretch, but they committed to it, celebrated it, and made it work.

It was a smart play. It was even wiser given the fact that Dunkin' made sure they were set up to execute it. The "America Runs on Dunkin'" campaign led to major brand success, growth, and expansion. It was all about delivering quick service that keeps you running, along with addictive quality coffee. I went all in, and I wasn't alone among the millions of people became celebrators of the Dunkin' brand.

The story flourished because the "America Runs on Dunkin'" concept was based on the most inspiring aspects of their brand. They were made to execute this race, and they ran it well.

In 2013, Dunkin' started running in a different direction, introducing a lineup of freshly brewed espresso, lattes, and cappuccinos. Shifting into the coffee business's specialty side was a logical next step that made perfect sense ... in theory. But the specialty drink focus resulted in store-level execution and quality issues. The shift was too much, too fast.

If your head is nodding as you read this, then you were one of the Dunkin' brand celebrators who felt like the company tried too hard to live the Starbucks story instead of easing into these changes. When promoting iced coffees, lattes, and highly detailed espresso drinks, you need to do more than buy a machine, give the drink a cool name, and put together a clever marketing campaign. Your operations have to be set up to deliver.

Through the "America Runs on Dunkin'" campaign, people had bonded with the company's story of having consistent, grab-'n-go, blue-collar-quality coffee. They changed the game and intentionally raised the stakes by choosing to run a different race that made their labor more intense and their training more time-consuming. In addition, the featured drink formula stepped away from its solid blue-collar focus. They began competing in a race designed for Starbucks-type businesses. They couldn't win.

A REQUIRED RESPONSE TO THE SHIFT

Dunkin' would have liked to have sold their lunch-bucket, blue-collar coffee forever. But the market that Starbucks made pushed American tastes upscale. Even McDonald's dove in the arena, offering fancy McCafé espressos, lattes, and cappuccinos. Dunkin's business would have been in serious trouble had it ignored these trends.

As a Dunkin' brand celebrator, I selfishly would have loved to see them continue to celebrate their quality, timeliness, consistency, and blue-collar mentality. But then the story got cluttered, and I struggled to bond and connect with the new version of the Dunkin' story.

An adjustment period, a new ad agency, and a change in leadership afforded a brand story resurgence. New leadership figured out how to offer the drinks America demands while bringing their operations back in alignment with the "America Runs on Dunkin'" promise. Their story celebration is back in high gear, and the future is bright for the Dunkin' brand.

It was such a remarkable comeback that in November 2018, *QSR Magazine* recognized Dunkin' as the year's "Most Transformational Brand." The article illustrates how the company is back to comprehensively celebrating their story and executing in a way that Dunkin' CMO (Chief Marketing Officer) Tony Weisman calls "Dunkin'-like fashion." That's a great quote because it showcases the importance they give to aligning their actions in accordance with the brand's associated expectations.

It also shows that Dunkin' is clearly focused on bringing pride back to the experience. The speed and value that customers loved went back into the experience through the implementation of ideas like a new handcrafted espresso machine, an eight-beverage tap system, and a first of its kind drive-through dedicated to mobile orders. They regrouped and recaptured brand story strength by taking the time to develop a plan in line with their identity and executing it with excellence. They got back to their story roots with what one Dunkin' franchisee told *QSR Magazine* was "nothing short of a 360 degree culture change."

A BRAND SHIFT IS MORE THAN WORDS

This example illustrates the complexities associated with brand shifting. Change happens, but you still have to respect the most inspiring parts of your brand. When building new ideas and programs with brand story alignment at the top of your mind from the start, you won't have to coordinate a Herculean comeback story like Dunkin' to get back on track. You'll be able to move swifter, stronger, and with more certainty because your story will give you strength from the start.

An essential vision of where you want to be in the future is required, because change is inevitable in every industry. But also realize that your relationships have been developed through impressions that your brand celebrators associate with your story. As passionate supporters, they will tolerate shift and change, but this has to be managed properly, to make sense with the story, and be planned for accordingly. To ensure that your brand can maintain connection with your story under any circumstance, you have to understand, respect, and value your delivery impressions. With this perspective, your company can transition in a way that makes sense and will be understood by your celebrators.

START WHERE YOU ARE

The process of Culture Development Marketing puts the importance of your impressions first. The mechanism begins with a quest to understand the brand's dominant perceptions.

People see brand impressions most vividly. Impressions have the most power, carry the greatest weight, and will connect to make the strongest effect. If you want to gain the attention of the people who matter most, align your story with the ideas that matter most. The power in brand development lies in the initial understanding of these earned attributes.

Pinpointing the right connections isn't an automatic process. A single brand may have thousands of cultural impressions. This overwhelming presence can make identifying the most inspiring aspects of the brand a challenge. A plan and a process for gaining this perspective are in order.

REVEAL YOUR REPUTATION: THE IMPRESSION ANALYSIS

A few years ago, I was part of a monthly CEO forum speaker series and was invited to attend a presentation of another speaker in that series. The lecturer was Mike Staver, author of the book *Leadership Isn't for Cowards*, who was addressing a room filled with CEOs and business leaders. In his presentation, he asked the leadership group, "How many of you think that employees are talking about you right now?"

He looked around at a mixed response of raised and unraised hands and stated, "If your hand did not go up, you're wrong." After the audience laughed, he continued.

"We are all getting talked about ... every one of us, because that is what people do. You have to **embrace** the fact that employees are talking about you, and you need to know what they are saying and the impression you are making."

The importance of understanding your impressions was present in his final words of advice: "If you have not had some sort of assessment to uncover what people are saying about you, you need to make that a top priority." I loved his enthusiasm for this exercise, and I agree wholeheartedly. A brand story celebration isn't about who you think you are, or who you want to be. It needs to begin with your reputation.

An Impression Analysis is your starting point for CDM. Before we dig into the mechanics of the analysis, know that there are many ways to view the word **impression** in business. In this process, the word **impression** refers to the feelings or opinions that resonate from the brand. Extract the brand's most dominant impressions to isolate the way the brand connects, understand where value is being delivered, and recognize the type of reputation being earned.

THIS IS FULL CIRCLE, NOT JUST ONE PERSON'S OPINION

We do a 360° Impression Analysis to extract input from all different types of people and reveal the perspectives that completely surround the brand. From first impressions made on less familiar participants to lasting impressions made on highly involved participants, you must understand the way your brand is perceived in every stage of the brand relationship. The goal is to determine the most dominant associations that shine through all those stages. By mapping the brand's impressions from a variety of perspectives, we can see what areas unmistakably sparkle.

Be intentional when you create your list of Impression Analysis participants, which is critical. Divide your data groups into internal and external participants.

Your Internal List:	Your External List:
Management	New Clients/Customers
Team Members	Established Clients/Customers
Vendors	Past Clients/Customers
Suppliers	
Partners	
Family Members	

The goal is an even response rate. We have found that the external list will have a response rate that is three to four times lower than your internal list, so be sure to target three to four times the number of external participants. This list-building approach will help ensure that you gain individual perspectives from various vantage points.

To have an accurate picture, see relationships at every level. Everything counts. If participants have an idea of what the brand is about, you want to know their reaction.

The exercise involves presenting the participants with a list of around 120 personal values and attributes. To get a clear and useful picture, include both positive and negative traits. We add and subtract terms for every assessment based on the person, company, or brand, but 90 percent of the list remains constant. The list of values and attributes should include personal, descriptive terms that people can associate with the brand.

For many businesses, using personal attributes in the analysis may seem out of place. However, before you remove them from the list, consider that personal attributes are easy associations and can be critical components of building trust and initiating relationships.

A list of personal values and attributes is available at EveryoneIsAnInfluencer.com/Impression, along with an explanation of a reverse-valuation process that can be used to measure your results. You can download the list and information using the password **brandstoryexpert**.

The list isn't a print-and-implement document. Examine the attributes, and add and subtract items to personalize it for your business or industry. The range that works best is a total number between 100–130 personal values and attributes.

The primary goal of the Impression Analysis is to become aware of the highest-ranked impressions. You can observe the ideas that resonate the most from a completed list, and notice patterns, affirm areas of connection, and recognize areas of disconnect.

—

INSIGHT OPENS UP OPPORTUNITY.

—

Mapping consistencies, connecting ideas, and recognizing patterns allow you to build a list of key insights from the Impression Analysis. I chart these observations by keeping "connection notes" through the procedure. They allow you to track your observations at this and every stage of the CDM process.

Record observations of authentic behavior and recognized patterns, which give you the perspective you need to uncover the story and storylines. You aren't creating this story—you are uncovering it. The goal is to graduate from a cluttered and disconnected vision to a clear and concise story. The insight and ideas generated through this exercise will enable you to connect the dots.

> You aren't creating this story—you are uncovering it.

REVEALING, NOT INVENTING

This path brings the story to you. Remember, revealing, not inventing, your story is important. Get input from every analysis section to ensure that the story doesn't form into a single-sided story or a management-made initiative. The Impression Analysis provides a broad perspective by highlighting the attributes that uncover undeniable influence. The results can confirm a brand's thoughts and beliefs of who they are, or some insight and knowledge can be gained about undervalued, overlooked, or unseen perspectives.

In late 2019, a client in Indianapolis had a leadership team that was convinced that their community involvement was a defining area of their brand. Why wouldn't it be? They had a long tradition of community involvement and it had always been an internal priority. They also spent a lot of money helping individuals and organizations in the community, giving away scholarships and so much more. It had to be recognized.

But it wasn't. The Impression Analysis results showed that the attribute "Community Oriented" didn't make the top fifteen. In fact, it barely made the top thirty.

The brand leaders were sure that their community efforts were being recognized, valued, and appreciated, but something was amiss. Our Impression Analysis helped us dig deeper, ultimately uncovering a key area of disconnect. Years prior they had chosen to subtly house their community efforts under a new program name. It was created to spotlight their community efforts in a way that didn't seem self-serving—an inconspicuous way to highlight their efforts. But it was so inconspicuous that nobody tied the community efforts back to the brand. Everything they were doing was going unnoticed.

The knowledge we gained allowed us to fix the issue with a more transparent community involvement approach. The team got on board and took pride in the efforts, while also allowing the public to pick up on their impact. The results were quick and easy to see. They began gaining a tremendous amount of respect and appreciation from radio, television, newspaper, and social media channels. Soon after the shift, they began benefitting from earned media stories showcasing and celebrating their community involvement. They didn't alter what they were doing; they simply started celebrating their efforts, and after a short time, their community-oriented image was (and still is) rightfully respected and appreciated.

If this company had only used the brand leaders' perspectives, they would have determined that they were doing a great job of building a

"Community Oriented" reputation. They were certainly spending the time and committing the resources. So why make changes?

Without this exercise, they would have continued to promote their community efforts in a confusing fashion because it seemed right. However, the awareness gained through the Impression Analysis gave them an expanded vision for a stronger story.

CUT THE CLUTTER

The Impression Analysis will not only amplify your awareness but also enable you to focus on the most important impressions. Once completed, you become more attentive to the outlined impressions, your insight is enhanced, and you begin to notice the presence of these aspects everywhere.

You may be asking yourself, "If I will see these attributes and notice these impressions everywhere, why do I need this process to identify them? Aren't they obvious?"

Unfortunately, nothing is clear and obvious without insight, knowledge, and understanding. As the "Community Oriented" example illustrates, a brand story cannot be constructed based on assumptions. This process confirms strengths and significance. When you understand the value of impressions, they shift to a more prominent place and take priority. The new positioning builds an elevated awareness, which is known as **perceptual vigilance**.

Have you ever been made aware of a word and then suddenly you hear or read it everywhere? Research a car that you are passionate about purchasing and you begin seeing that car on every trip you take? That is **perceptual vigilance:** a process in which a person notices and recognizes the stimuli that are more significant to them. It's automatic.

The Impression Analysis creates this type of stimuli with the wisdom to identify and prioritize the brand's most inspiring aspects. You become aware of how those ideas are making the most impact on your audience, noticing how they relate to each other and beginning to see the value in their presence.

Perceptual vigilance can't define a story on its own. However, the insight gained from this first step is critical to the success of the entire process. It initiates development by revealing the most dominant impressions. It isolates focus on these brand-inspiring elements, helping you recognize and appreciate each earned impression. You gain understanding, awareness, and appreciation of how these ideas impact the brand.

This wisdom is required to help pinpoint defining statements in the next R.A.C.E. step, where you will evaluate a survey of a brand's core components in the Assessment phase.

ARMED AND READY TO ASSESS

When you enter the Assessment phase, you are armed with a perspective and an awareness of the brand's most inspiring attributes. These are the insights and ideas that set you up to map connections while reviewing your survey answers. Your heightened perspective allows you gain a much clearer vision of how the outlined impressions are being earned. The notes, perspective, and awareness gained in the Reveal Stage are a first step that will not only help you pull the story together but also become a valuable content development resource in the future.

The next chapter will continue to review the R.A.C.E. by taking a look at the assessment's origin to understand how it works, who it works for, and why it works so well in moving this process toward a successful brand celebration.

SUMMARY:

- The process of CDM helps you understand who you are and how your company is being perceived by isolating the ways you deliver value.

- CDM consists of uncovering your brand story, working the information down from its broadest perspective to its tightest definition.

- Focusing on running a race that lines up with your talents and abilities, will allow you to do more, be more, and go further.

- The goal is to graduate from a cluttered and disconnected vision to a clear and concise story.

CHAPTER EIGHT

Your Story Won't Save a Sinking Ship

I MAGINE A HOUSEWARMING party in which the guests are greeted with a laundry-filled living room, a kitchen stacked with two weeks of dirty dishes, and the aroma of a busted sewer line. You might "spread the word," but not in a good way. Negative experiences would dominate, and the gathering would not be a celebration.

It's the same way with CDM. You don't want your story to be dominated by the negative aspects of your brand. You need to be aware of the negative aspects of your brand, but you don't need to trumpet them. The goal of CDM is to uncover the most inspiring aspects of the story so they can take center stage. Identifying these areas enables you to spotlight the way the brand acts, how it performs, and the results it delivers. You are showcasing and celebrating these positive attributes in a real and relatable way so they can be easily seen, understood, and appreciated.

A company doesn't need to be perfect for a story celebration to occur. There will be some areas—sometimes big ones—where progress and improvement are needed. However, before you invest time, effort, and money into brand story development, you need to be confident that the company is functional, not fractured.

As you uncover and weigh the impact of the positive aspects of the brand experience, take note of the presence and impact of brand deficiencies. The scorecard happens naturally and is easy to tally. If the end result indicates that the brand's inspiring aspects outweigh the negative, then your functional brand is ready for a story celebration. However, if the outcome of the exercise illustrates a dysfunctional brand, not ready for celebration, that understanding needs to be accepted. A story can't force a brand to be functional. "Looking for the good" does not mean putting your head in the sand. My career path helped me learn this lesson early.

In the summer of 1994, I was starting my first job out of college—entering the workforce. I lived in my home state of Ohio and traveled down the river to my new job as the Director of Advertising for 37 Convenient Food Mart (CFM) stores operating in the Ohio Valley region.

After entering the building, I was ushered upstairs for my first meeting with a regional office owner. He managed the advertising in the past and was eager to show me the ropes. He started the conversation with a handshake, a few jokes, and a quick history lesson. The key insight was that our regional office was part of a struggling national CFM franchise group. The CFM system was fragmented, and the whole franchise was a bit of a mess.

Less than a decade ago, the CFM franchise was the nation's third-largest chain of convenience stores, operating nearly 20 regional offices with over 1,200 US stores. Then ownership at the national office rotated multiple times, systems changed, follow-through went out the window, and the franchise shrank to seven regional headquarters and around 400 stores.

The news got worse. Franchisees felt that the CFM national office advertising programs were a joke. The regional office owner explained that few store owners saw value in the advertising program, and the advertising meeting attendance was anemic. Nobody was participating and tensions were high. He finished by saying, "Yep, that's where we're at." Then he laughed. "If you want to leave now, you can."

I chuckled, but I never thought about leaving. He did me a huge favor by providing an accurate depiction of what I was up against, so instead of focusing on the negative, I began looking for the good. I didn't concern myself with issues that were out of my control. I focused on my job, which was to deliver value to the store owners. The first priority was meeting every store owner, understanding their needs, and building relationships with them.

Each visit to a store became an opportunity to learn about the business, understand how each store operated, and recognize the most inspiring aspects of the company.

As my visits added up and began to make an impact, advertising meeting attendance increased. It was progress in motion as more owners joined in discussions regarding the formation of sales plans and store offerings. Their participation sparked collective input, and their ideas came to life through collaborative program development.

GAINING MOMENTUM

The first project we put together was a food service program that bundled offerings from Coca-Cola and Frito Lay with store-made chicken and wings. I called the deal the "Monster Tailgate Package," and nearly all of the owners agreed to participate. We set a price, designed a marketing plan, and secured some all-pro influencers to promote the package.

The first year's influencer was former Pittsburgh Steeler and NFL Hall of Fame running back Franco Harris. A few years later, I negotiated a partnership with Steeler defensive back Rod Woodson, another Hall of Fame player who was still playing with the Steelers. Both players agreed to commercials and print ads to promote the Monster Tailgate Package. The project was a success: a consistent program, high-profile endorsers, and a quality presentation. While it didn't solve the marketing problem, it certainly made a splash, and we were making progress!

The next food service program was a huge fish sandwich with long, extended crisscrossed filets. I called it the "Big Catch One Pound Fish Sandwich." The signature sandwich sold over 67,000 fish sandwiches in its first year during Lent. The sandwich itself became an eye-popping influencer, with billboards featuring conspicuous filets that extended beyond the board. The sandwich was a huge hit.

We kept working to plan and execute consistent programs and promotions throughout the stores. Participation grew each time. Slowly but surely, the CFM Ohio Valley regional office began building a reputation for engagement and innovation. Soon, CFM regionals in other markets who were struggling with participation took notice, and I began working with multiple regions while unity built. I even developed a full company category conference where vendors, partners, and owners from every CFM region traveled abroad to improve communication, understanding, and appreciation.

At this point, I was ready to work with clients in different industries, so I created my own ad agency and brought the CFM regionals on as clients. I worked with these fantastic franchise owners as clients for over a decade. I treasure my time with these store owners, and I take great pride in the dozens of programs we developed together, in partnership with their vendors.

But in the end, the makeup of their business ultimately made it a bittersweet relationship.

—

WORDS ALONE CAN'T FIX THE
FOUNDATIONS OF A RELATIONSHIP.

—

I had done all I could to bring the best out of each regional office and help the individual store owners. Our programs generated a buzz in the industry through the innovative programs we developed and through our influencer partnerships. Interviews in trade journals, serving on national advisory boards, and building relationships led to amazing experiences, even traveling to the Summer Olympics in Sydney, Australia, with Coca-Cola. I had looked for and found the good in this job. Unfortunately, the company had a core story problem that couldn't be remedied.

The franchise relationship was ill, and issues beyond my influence poisoned the story from the start. I loved these store owners and I wanted to build their story even bigger. Still, there are limitations to what Culture Development Marketing can do. CFM was simply not a functional organization. Working with these stores helped me to realize that brand story development is not a process for fixing a dysfunctional organization.

The realization was not a negative outcome ... it was a breakthrough. It narrowed my focus, making it easier to identify the right partnerships for the process. I began to look closer, learn more, and take a more systematic approach.

The game-changing takeaway I received from CFM is this:

> Culture Development Marketing isn't about taking a dysfunctional brand to functional. Its power lies in helping a functional brand elevate to optimal.

This understanding flipped the switch: The process is not for everyone, and I had to understand why.

A dysfunctional brand can't create long-term, meaningful changes through CDM. People simply don't want to celebrate a broken culture. A dysfunctional brand is a far better candidate for an Operational Evaluation, where the end result can help reconstruct and reorganize its business into a functional format.

COACHING IS NOT THERAPY

CDM's inability to take a dysfunctional brand to functional is served by a good analogy between the coaching process and the practice of therapy.

The process of coaching as a methodology is designed to bring out the best. It results in an awareness that allows a person or company to recognize who they are and how they can operate to their fullest potential. Coaches bring out your best by working to help you uncover ideas that you may be overlooking, enabling you to see what is already within you in a new and inspiring way. *The goal of the coach is to elevate you from functional to optimal.* Therefore, if you are severely damaged, the coaching process probably isn't the ideal first step for you.

Therapy is a strong solution for diagnosing and resolving problematic beliefs, behaviors, issues, and feelings. The goal of a therapist is geared toward aiding the transition from dysfunctional to functional to help you create a happier and more stable future.

These comparisons demonstrate how the process of CDM is similar to coaching. A clear link exists between the informal strategies I had been using since the beginning of my marketing career and the foundational principles of coaching. Diving into the coaching process on a deeper level would reveal if dedicated training in the field of coaching would enable me to formalize my mechanism for brand story development. I invested in a program with the Institute for Professional Excellence in Coaching.

The deeper my knowledge about the principles of coaching, the more certain I became that this information would help me uncover insights, gain clarity, and systemize a process for taking brands from functional to optimal.

Functional brands that aren't celebrating the story are on the cusp of greatness. These companies have unique and inspiring aspects at work, but that story isn't getting told. The right questions aren't being asked to summarize and showcase the true reputation they have earned. As a result, they just blend in.

The next R.A.C.E. step is the Assessment phase: how asking the right questions unlocks the power to extract the story that matters most, setting you up to educate and inspire the people who matter most. It's the secret to building an army of influencers.

HOW TO EXECUTE A BRAND STORY SURVEY

Building a relevant Brand Story Survey is critical so you can start to close the gap between what your brand is and what your brand could be—and to make the best results happen more often.

1. Establish a safe environment so leaders can discuss the strengths and weaknesses of the brand.

2. Choose both brand leaders and other stakeholders.

3. Use **targeted questions** to develop an understanding of your brand.

4. Highlight the themes that appear in different people's answers.

DON'T LOOK FOR WHAT YOU WANT TO HEAR ... LOOK FOR WHAT'S GOOD AND REAL

Whether it's a business talking to customers through marketing channels or a parent talking to a 13-year-old child at the dinner table, one of the most natural conversational tendencies is the overwhelming urge to drive the narrative toward the story you want to hear.

Consciously or subconsciously, we ask questions to get the answers we want, and we lead the discussion in a way that suits our needs. The problem with this type of query is that the information exchanged is predetermined, forced, and inauthentic.

The process of CDM isn't designed to put ideas in someone's mind, but to pull great information out. You don't steer the conversation, implant ideas, or guide others to accomplish a predetermined end result. There can be no right or wrong answers to the questions in the Connection Map, which is intended to be an organic and natural process based on discovery. The map is not the territory.

Create an open environment through well-thought-out questions to facilitate the sharing of insights and ideas. This is the mindset needed when creating the questions for your Connection Map.

Structure the questions to allow the story to reveal itself. The goal of the map is to build a list of questions for a group of 2–4 brand leaders who possess a heightened perspective of the brand.

You already have a comprehensive, high-level evaluation of the brand through the Impression Analysis, so you don't require endless input. Only a few key individuals are needed to help you understand how the outlined impressions have been earned. It's all about asking the right questions to the right people.

For the survey, you will construct a series of open-ended questions that will build a dialogue around Attitude, Drive, and Direction. Elicit insight into the way the brand acts and feels, how it operates and performs, and what it does to earn the reputation and outcomes detailed in the Impression Analysis. When considering the questions, plan out what you'll ask to achieve the following strategic goals.

To create an understanding of the organizational attitudes that exist:

You may consider asking questions like ...

- "What is the mentality that's driving our brand to be successful?"
- "What is our brand passionate about accomplishing?"
- "What gets the team excited?"
- "What's it like being a part of this company and culture?"

To allow the answerer to detail the habits, systems, and processes that Drive brand success:

You may consider asking questions like ...

- "When do you feel our brand is operating at its best?"
- "What systems or processes differentiate us from competitors?"
- "What actions power our brand to be successful?"
- "What core systems, processes, or standards contribute most to our identity?"

To generate conversation about the results and reputation the Drive the brand:

You may consider asking questions like ...

- "What is our brand known for the most?"
- "What does our brand help our clients/customers accomplish?"
- "What does our brand specifically do that makes us a leader in our industry?"
- "What is the main goal for our brand, and what do you do to be certain this goal is achieved?"

Make the questions feel natural, and provide the freedom to answer in a real, relatable, and authentic way. Develop questions using brand language that people are familiar with and understand. This isn't a test, so make it easy and automatic.

—

REMEMBER: YOU WANT ALL THE INFO.
EVEN YOUR CHALLENGES.

—

Put the brand leaders at ease by explaining that this exercise isn't about providing the correct answer ... it's about answering every question in a way that feels natural. Open, honest, instinctive answers will provide the information you require to connect the dots and summarize the story.

Design your Brand Story Survey questions using the component areas to draft an intentional order:

- First, craft a set of questions for uncovering Attitude.

- Then, create a different set of questions aimed at uncovering Drive.

- Finally, devise a third set of questions concerning Direction.

Keep in mind that a multitude of questions can be asked, but you don't want to exhaust the brand leaders taking the evaluation. Aim for 6–8 questions at most in each area. You can execute the assessment through an online survey, or through a recorded and transcribed phone interview. Either way, the completed assessment will provide you with the information to move on to the next step.

CONNECTION MAPPING: CONNECTING THE GOOD WITH THE REAL

Just as the three core components of the story work together to do something greater, the steps in the process of Culture Development Marketing work together to achieve more as well. Each stage sets up the next. A defined path will allow the process to result in awareness, open up new perspectives, and forge clarity. Remember to focus on following the outlined order of the R.A.C.E steps. Intentional, step-by-step implementation is critically important.

When you begin by revealing the most inspiring aspects of the brand through the Impression Analysis, you generate the perceptual vigilance needed to execute the Brand Story Survey. In contrast, if you were to read the survey answers first, you would not have the same level of clarity, understand the weight of each answer, or be able to accurately assess the value of the information and ideas. We call it a map because we are looking to reveal the territory, not create the territory.

In following the steps, the results of the Impression Analysis are at the forefront of your thoughts as you read over the survey answers. Then use the survey answers to connect the dots of how these impressions are being earned. When reviewing the answers, take connection notes—underlining essential points, circling key words, and highlighting critical findings. Respect every connection you feel and trust your instincts. Your mind may be trying to tell you something that you aren't yet ready to learn.

Record your impulse observations and map perceptual vigilance. Every feeling matters, because these observations are jumping out at you for a reason. Even if you don't understand the rationale at the time, record the thought to the best of your ability. Connection notes can group with other ideas to open your eyes to a fresh perspective. Understand the way the defined impressions operate inside the brand, how your business is earning these impressions, and what they mean to the overall brand experience. Write them down so you have that information available for later use.

IT'S TIME TO ORGANIZE AND PRIORITIZE

When you are done evaluating the answers from the leaders whom you chose to take the Brand Story Survey and you have all the related connection notes, it's time to begin organizing your ideas. Look at brand language patterns, concept consistencies, illustrations of a shared mindset, related power statements, and more. The story will start to take shape as you group these ideas into a working summary. At first, you may have a summary that is several paragraphs long, or have to draft multiple versions, but just go with what feels natural.

Sometimes it takes an hour to condense your summary into a paragraph, while other times it may take two days before you feel it's just right. Don't put pressure on the process. Simply step away when the task is becoming too daunting. Keep in mind that this exercise is not about getting it done; it's about getting it right.

When you feel good about your summary, check to make sure you have included the three core elements of the story:

- Attitude ... convey the personal and emotional way your brand connects

- Drive ... so the systems and processes that power the brand are recognized

- Direction ... to initiate a purposeful mindset through the understanding of where the brand experience will lead

Aim to finish with a single paragraph that, in most cases, will be 50–80 words in length. Shorter or longer summaries may be right for the brand. However, 50–80 words gives you a target for a solid, comprehensive summary.

LESS IS MORE: DON'T OVEREXPLAIN

We all have a natural tendency to overexplain with too much content. For that reason, the act of refining is usually less about adding ideas and more about simplification. You've arrived at a final brand story summary when you have trimmed it to the point where it still tells the whole story and you wouldn't feel comfortable removing any additional words or content.

Constructing an authentic brand story summary takes energy, effort, and concentrated thinking. The R.A.C.E. steps may uncover the story, but you cannot race through defining your story too quickly. Again, the process takes time and has to be done correctly. Time and commitment are two of the main reasons that most companies don't go through this type of process.

Perhaps another reason is because they don't feel like they need a comprehensive brand narrative. A decade ago, the whole idea of expressing the intricacies of who you were and what your values were to the customers was considered irrelevant. But your clear brand story is what makes you relevant. Brands who celebrate their story are the standouts.

—

PEOPLE ARE CRAVING REAL.

—

People want real talk. They crave to tap into the full story that allows them to relate and bond with their personal ideas and interests. Your well-defined, comprehensive brand story forges this bond. It's authentic, it's powerful, and it's comprehensive, but before you showcase it, you have to create a plan to support it.

Now that we have discussed creating a brand story summary, we will move on to the final stage of the R.A.C.E.—building a framework to celebrate your story.

SUMMARY:

- Look for the good: The most inspiring aspects of the brand are the stars of the story.
- A brand story celebration cannot make a dysfunctional brand functional.
- Focus on functional to optimal.
- Keep it real.

CHAPTER NINE

Creating a Framework for Celebration

A T THE BEGINNING of this book, we stressed how critical it is for brands to avoid talking shit. Nobody will believe you anyway, so why bother? A brand celebration helps you avoid this pitfall by generating real, authentic, and meaningful content. It spotlights aspects, examples, and instances that back up your story.

These inspired illustrations set up an inspirational energy that elevates your brand, making you distinct from other companies.

However, a brand story can't create a celebration if it feels forced. You want people to be inspired to join in, so you have to plan and identify a purpose. The next step in this process is about charting that course. Taking your newfound awareness, connection notes, and clear brand story summary and using them to generate a content plan not only lift the brand in celebration but also ensure the party keeps going.

ELEVATE YOUR BRAND | CELEBRATE YOUR STORY

Your brand story summary constructed a clear vision of the most inspiring aspects of your brand through a combination of relatable language, earned ideas, and thoughtful structure. It set up the opportunity to create a brand celebration with content that educates people on who the brand is and what makes it special. The statement sets you apart by multiplying key brand story behaviors to bring your brand story to life. It's a powerful paragraph.

While the impact of your summary is enormous, it cannot reach out and connect on its own. It acts as the foundation for your brand story celebration by opening up the ability to create subset content that reaches out to connect, inspire and educate. The power to create this type of content is harnessed around two instruments:

- A **Brand Story Title** that is short, meaningful, and memorable
- **Storylines** that are educational and engaging

Your brand story title and supporting storylines are the content tools needed to produce excitement, educate others, and build relationships. In this chapter, we will discuss the importance of your brand story title and associated storylines, and how these tools provide the fuel to establish an inspiring brand story celebration.

CRAFTING YOUR TITLE: NOT A SLOGAN

Don't confuse your brand story title with a slogan or tagline. A slogan is commonly used for a specific campaign or program and has a limited lifespan. A tagline is more similar to a brand story title, but many times taglines are product centric, transactional, and marketing driven. Your brand story title represents what a slogan is at its best: a culture-driven message that strengthens your image and works as a reinforcing agent for your brand story summary.

When you identify and craft your title, it becomes a meaningful mantra that showcases the most exciting

> Your brand story title represents what a slogan is at its best

aspects of the story and makes people want to know more. It stays in their mind by forming its own version of perceptual vigilance, helping consumers recall your brand image when triggered.

Your brand story title should work in combination with a brand story summary and storylines to organize roles, clarify what is being celebrated, and get the people who matter most involved in the process.

—

IT'S EASY TO NOTICE IN BOOKS AND MOVIES HOW A GOOD TITLE DRAWS YOU IN AND INSPIRES YOU TO LEARN MORE.

—

A good title can make or break a story. It catches your attention and sets the tone while leaving a lasting impression. You may not realize the impact it makes as it changes the way stories are received and remembered.

A good example of this is the 1990 classic film *Pretty Woman*. This unique love story holds a special place in people's hearts for the way the story was connected in such a fun and romantic way. However, the original title was *3,000*, representing the amount of money Richard Gere paid Julia Roberts. That's not nearly as memorable … or romantic.

Even when the story is the same, titles matter.

A title is a valuable part of the plan in constructing a brand story celebration. However, it is not a stand-alone instrument that constructs clarity on its own. Your brand story title is a device that clearly directs people to the most inspiring aspects of the story. It is the impetus that brings people in and inspires them to want to know more. It acts as a reinforcing agent that triggers the remembrance of the brand story and solidifies its message. When developing your title, be certain it sparks interest and understanding by relating and referring to the brand story summary in a memorable way.

The ideal length for a title is generally five words or under, and many believe that the shorter it is, the better it will be. With that said, it may end up longer, but ensure that it doesn't try to do too much. When people attempt to convey too many messages, they end up making no points at all. A simple and smart title will reflect the brand's personality.

Allstate's "You're in good hands with Allstate" provides a strong slogan that functions as a brand title. These six words refer to a complete story of the brand experience and its benefits. Allstate's brand title goes far beyond the realm of a typical slogan because it promotes their culture by defining a strong and trustworthy attitude, a driving commitment to customers, and the purposeful promise of the security they deliver. When companies use their title to activate their brand story in this manner, they take control of their story, ensuring that this tool will function to continually celebrate the expectations associated with the brand experience.

TITLES: NO RULES, JUST RIGHT!

Many marketers want to set strict rules, such as "Slogans and taglines should never contain a period" or that they "should be expressed in five words or less." These ideas may be useful benchmarks, not iron-clad rules to dictate your final decision. They're only guidelines for consideration while you refine your message.

The most important rule in CDM is that when it comes to the development of your title and storylines, make sure that every piece of the puzzle connects. If you do this, you can break the other rules. If there were a rule to forbid titles from possessing periods, four of the top titles in history would never have been invented. You would never have seen Nike's "Just Do It." or Apple's "Think Different." or Avis's "We Try Harder." or "Don't leave home without it." from American Express.

Furthermore, if the "five words or less" rule were strictly enforced, Federal Express would have unwisely reduced their wildly successful title "When it absolutely, positively has to be there overnight" to something simple and plain like "the Overnight Delivery Company." If you feel a period is needed to anchor the line, or to create a sense of finality, leave it. If you think trimming your title to get it to five words or less will cut out the heart of your message, don't trim it. Go with what feels right as a messenger for the complete story and be certain it connects.

Nike, Apple, Avis, American Express, and FedEx are just a few brands that use effective brand story titles to tell their story. The best brands understand how to use their title to drive people to want to know more about the brand. Their title is a reinforcement agent that celebrates their values and beliefs while setting up the expectations associated with the brand and providing the opportunity to connect. When a company values their story and supports it with a well-targeted title and inspiring storyline, watching them navigate through the celebration of their story is like witnessing effortless art.

BUILDING A STORY HELPS YOUR COMMUNITY CONNECT FASTER

Your clearly defined brand story summary provides a comprehensive overview that spans the entire brand experience, and your brand story title frames the story. Storylines are subsets that open up and expand the narrative, providing the framework for brand education and content creation.

The most effective storyline opportunities are built around concepts that allow the brand to illustrate different story aspects. When you use storylines to focus in on specific segments, you enable interested people to see the story from different perspectives, multiplying the connection opportunities.

Storylines inspire content creation, clearly identifying a concentrated theme to support brand story promotion, education, and celebration. By providing storylines, the brand takes a leadership role, outlining the key aspects of the brand story and promoting them in a coordinated fashion.

Storylines are critical because you can develop content centered on celebrating your story in different ways, targeting a variety of groups and audiences. Each storyline becomes a brand education initiative. This guidance means that your team never has to worry about figuring out what type of content is relevant. Your brand story summary and storylines illustrate what they need to know to take part in the celebration.

Storylines open up opportunities for team members, customers, and community members to recognize their role and participate in celebrating the brand story. Integration opportunities can be easily identified, as these storyline subsets allow the brand to look beyond the typical endorsement process to add new characters and unique stories into the celebration of the brand.

Storylines make it easy to see that great stories surround us. CDM arms you with the insight, knowledge, and awareness to go beyond the norm to produce timeless stories that make a real and lasting impact.

THE STRENGTH OF A GOOD STORYLINE

This example happened over a decade ago, but it still rings true.

In 2010, most health and fitness clubs were engaging in a competitive war on membership prices. As the price war escalated to an unhealthy level, Gold's Gym decided to run their own race. They focused on the story that they had earned during 45 years of powerful business strategies. The primary impression was "strength." So Gold's Gym set out to define the story behind that impression. The storyline they devised was "Know Your Own Strength." The story was defined to illustrate that the company's focus wasn't on muscle heads or membership fees. Gold's Gym was about building strength in people's lives.

Gold's activated the "Know Your Own Strength" storyline with signage, a tracking app, commercials, and a social media piece for collecting people's own "Strong Stories." They even encouraged sharing on Twitter, tagging posts with #strongerthan and a variety of related hashtags. A series of three documentaries that told individual "Strong Stories" through their own members caught my attention. The stories were directed by award-winning documentarian Eliott Rausch. Each video clarified a Gold's customer's experience from different perspectives.

These videos demonstrated how getting fit became a positive force that gave people strength in different ways. One video told the account of Erin, who lost her house in the recession and gained her confidence and energy back through exercise. Her story was relevant, relatable, and inspiring. The second video related the story of Jim, an overweight man who needed to lose enough weight to be medically able to donate a kidney to his sick wife. This story detailed the impact of family illness with a heroic twist. Finally, my all-time favorite brand story video was the tale of 96-year-old Harry and his goal of staying active to make the century mark. (See the video at EveryoneIsAnInfluencer.com/Harry.)

You might expect to see a commercially produced story explaining how getting fit at Gold's Gym gave Harry energy, or how Harry's Gold's Gym trainer helped him feel alive at 96. The video did show that, but there was much more. Being in tune with the inspiring aspects of the Gold's Gym brand story gave the videographer the ability to define his strength uniquely and memorably.

As the video progresses, we see the expected path of presenting the trainer's value being brought to Harry's life. Then Harry talks about his views on life and his passion for helping young people. It blends right into the trainer talking about his admiration for Harry. However, as the trainer continues to speak, you begin to realize that his relationship with Harry goes beyond setting goals and ensuring he gets enough reps. A unique relationship is unfolding.

As Harry's voiceover states, "There's always someone out there who needs you," the unmistakable joy in this short video emerges. It shifts to illustrate what the trainer needs and how he's is inspired by Harry.

The spirit of the 96-year-old man is motivating his trainer. It is a brand celebration masterpiece.

UNEXPECTED INFLUENCE

We expect creative personnel to present the trainer as the hero who set goals for the client. We also expect to see the client experience success and value through their participation at Gold's. But it's more than that—the story's power generating these two people to inspire each other is surprising. The storyline dials in on relationships and effectively presents them as the brand's inspirational aspect. This beautiful message is generated by a perfectly choreographed storyline strategy.

- The "Know Your Own Strength" storyline opened up the opportunity to conceptualize the "Strong Stories" series.

- The series identified members and trainers who could help educate and celebrate the storyline in a memorable way.

- The strategy created starring roles for unexpected influencers.

Gold's uncovered the story and went deeper than getting in shape or comparing membership rates. The brand dove into something far more real and relatable. It's a magical story that provides a moving look into the fulfilling and inspiring life of being a Gold's Gym trainer.

Through the Strong Stories series, the company successfully illustrated that they not only understand the deep relationships their trainers have with clients, but that the company is proud of those relationships. They recognize it as a distinguishable trait and are celebrating that part of their story with their customers and team members.

How many Gold's Gym trainers do you think can relate to that story? How many trainers were moved by that story? How many potential clients saw Gold's Gym trainers in a more positive light? The answer is: a lot.

A STRONG STORY CREATES STRONG MARGINS

In 2010, the big-box fitness centers were all locked in a death march to lower prices. They were engaging in the wrong race: a race to the bottom over pricing and services, and their margins were hurting.

To escape this death spiral, they couldn't just design more ads—they had to find leverage. It wasn't all about selling people on Gold's Gym. The storyline "Know Your Own Strength" was fresh and inspiring. They weren't running the same race by hawking memberships with a lowballed monthly fee; they were celebrating a story that highlighted the most inspiring aspects of the brand in every way.

This storyline accomplished specific goals and reached a desirable target audience through the power of passionate participation. The stories that were told created powerful influencers all around the brand. There were internal and external benefits of elevating the brand in this memorable way.

LIVE YOUR LIFE, CELEBRATE YOUR BRAND

As you highlight single stories as part of your brand celebration, you'll begin to see that the best storylines are the ones that can relate to specific segments of consumers. Be on the lookout for people and ideas that are aligned with the promise of the brand.

In branding, it has become cliché to say that the goal of a content plan is to "live the brand." This statement emphasizes telling someone to live a specific way. For that reason, I have never liked the comment. Living anything can't be a directive. Merely saying that you want to "live your brand" is not a rallying cry for a thriving content strategy. Systemizing something that should be natural and instinctive should never feel fake or phony. Deliberate celebrations don't request others to live your story, but to let them know of your pride in the reputation you have earned together and inspire them to celebrate that story with you.

Having a content plan centered on brand story education permits this deliberate approach, which will allow you to outline supporting storylines. These storylines build a framework for supportive content creation. Discovering these subset ideas breaks the story into manageable content projects, supporting clear expectations about what the brand is going to celebrate.

The art of onboarding eager individuals to celebrate your story has no set rules. Some brands communicate implied invitations through storylines that illustrate ways to connect with their story, while others may take a more deliberate storyline approach to onboarding celebrators.

VPX's Bang Energy drink company understands how storylines can develop long-term relationships centered on education and integration. The company celebrates their story in an inclusive way, with storylines surrounding three separate storyline focus areas:

- Promote scientific supplement studies that support Bang's various ingredients

- Educate on proper exercise techniques and supplement usage to position Bang Energy with a fit, energetic lifestyle

- Align an edgy, risqué lifestyle that celebrates, glamorizes, and promotes the use of Bang Energy products

Each of these storylines makes an impact. However, when you put them together, you discover that Bang is supplying their like-minded celebrators with all the energy they need to keep the Bang party going. Yes, this energy drink company has turned their controversial CEO Jack Owoc's catchphrase, "If you ain't Bangin' you ain't Hangin'," into an invitation for similar people to jump aboard Bang's brand story celebration. In fact, Bang makes it easy for those people to see how they fit in their story through their outlined Bang Influencer Affiliate program.

Like many influencer affiliate approaches, the main idea is to invite a person to become a Bang Influencer, who will then promote and support the brand on their social media channels. However, the Bang program goes a step further than most by clearly stating the type of influencer they want. The qualification page proudly states, "An Xtremely fit physique as well as an enthusiastic, outgoing personality are requirements for joining our team." They position the role of a Bang Influencer as status that you audition for—and hope to be awarded—and the public is going after the opportunity. Aspiring influencers want to be a part of that group so bad that they go all in by jumping through hoops to get there.

The comprehensive storyline approach led to a full stream of high-energy user-composed content and imagery from fitness models, fashion influencers, lifestyle bloggers, and active supporters on every social media channel. Bang Energy is gaining passionate paid and unpaid brand celebrators by the truckload, flooding Instagram and TikTok with #bangenergy influencer posts.

Storylines work best when they help people understand where they fit in, the ways they can make an impact, and how they can take part in the celebration. Establish roles and make it easy for others to find their way into the story. Brands can't just live the brand story and expect people to take notice; they have to shape a relatable celebration. That's how efforts become focused and powerful.

CHANGE IS INEVITABLE: BE PREPARED FOR IT

When you commit to executing a plan with multiple content goals and objectives, your messaging will evolve, engage, educate, and inspire. Storylines help similar people visualize their role in your business and provide additional opportunities for them to connect with content that they identify with personally. By increasing the number of connection opportunities, individuals inside and outside the brand can more easily see where they fit in with the story.

If you want to inspire a like-minded person to become a brand influencer, help them visualize their role, understand how they can contribute, and decide whether they want to be a part of the story. The goal of a brand story celebration is to make it easy for others to recognize these opportunities to relate and connect with the brand. Using your brand story as a decision-making mechanism to decide what ideas are worthy of your story will ensure the creation of compelling content that connects— even through situations like election upheaval or global pandemics.

The following checklist of steps will guide you in creating a framework for successful content creation in the celebration of your brand story.

- **Identify the Initiatives:** Develop storylines to showcase critical content objectives. They allow you to discover and plan content goals that celebrate supporting ideas in a way that impacts your customers, your company, and your culture. To create a content strategy, start by outlining actions that showcase exciting aspects of your brand, with ongoing and supporting content ideas, examples, and illustrations. These opportunities might consist of a hashtag strategy, a social video series, an annual event, a reoccurring posting plan, a blogging strategy, or an outlined plan to share knowledge. Each content initiative should effectively reinforce the targeted storyline, helping to build strength and support for the brand story.

- **Determine the Channels:** It is impossible to design a plan for every social media channel. The key to a great plan, then, is to examine each storyline design on its own. If a social media platform is a good fit to support the storyline, consider adding it to the program. Remember, you may want to target ten channels of support for execution, but can you execute all ten in a way that adds value? If the answer is a resounding yes, do it. If you have any doubt, cut back until you are certain that you can accomplish your plan in a way that honors the brand.

- **Outline the Outcome:** Determine the results you want to accomplish. Detail the attitude you want to communicate, the operational aspects you want to explain, and the outcomes you want to illustrate for the storylines. Each one needs an intentional purpose that is understood internally by your team. When you present that information, it puts employees, marketing staff, management, and more all on the same page. They will all benefit from this awareness, and it will increase your chances for engagement and success.

- **Set the Timing:** Each channel plan must contain expectations associated with timing. Pacing is an important factor in sharing content. Regardless of how passionate people are about your brand, they can only absorb so much. Don't underwhelm your audience, but don't overwhelm them either. Just be aware that pacing strategies continually evolve. Channels constantly change their algorithms, and what worked a week ago won't necessarily work this week. Monitor your content plan strategy and results frequently.

- **Create a System:** Determine a content sharing strategy. A decade ago, we adopted the idea that "celebrating your story is a team sport." It's a necessary mindset for success in celebrating your story. We first developed a mobile uploader for every client to automate that process. However, we kept building different versions of this tool until we built an app called "The All In App," which is a brand communication game changer. It makes the execution of Culture Development Marketing effective and easy. The app can be found at TheAllInApp.com, and it permits brands to gamify content sharing, streamlining participation and supporting the celebration with a consistent flow of real and authentic content. Without that content, you can't celebrate your story. Put simply, if you want to illustrate the way you back up your story to your customers, you need content from your team with a system that works.

- **Evaluate and Measure:** Continually evaluate the success of your program. Brand leaders want numbers, reports, and real results. You do too! Tools exist to measure success by analyzing engagement, follower-to-following ratio, geotags, hashtag use, and so much more. However, be careful that you don't get lost in the abundance of available information. Isolate the metrics that make the most sense to your brand and evaluate your efforts religiously.

EXECUTE WITH AN INFLUENCER

The process of CDM is simple and straightforward, but it is still a mechanism with execution and implementation that takes time, effort, and attention. Larger brands realize the need to commit to fully staffed internal and external marketing teams who work to celebrate their story. Most midsized organizations also realize the need to fully commit to execute and implement a vibrant social sharing program. Small brands are different. Some get it, while others struggle to realize the importance of celebrating their story. At any level, it's a mistake to undervalue the impact of your story celebration.

Brands must devote time and talent to execute the celebration in a way that resonates. When your media and messaging are led by half-committed people, the message is never believable. The audience feels slimy, like a shady salesman paid them an insincere compliment just to get their business.

For companies to get it right, they must realize that developing success takes an all-embracing onboarding strategy aimed at drawing people toward the brand. Don't half-ass the process and expect a person who plans and executes a content calendar for the month in 30 minutes to influence others. Make sure that anyone who represents your brand is a well-informed, passionate Brand Celebrator. You cannot create an army of Influencers for your brand if the people managing your brand messaging strategy are not card-carrying Influencers.

Too many brands produce low-quality content that viewers just want to go away. It's a trend fueled by disengaged social media managers who tackle content calendars with a "just get it done" mentality. Their content not only fails to educate, but it pisses people off. These "content-mill" social media workers crank out social posts for the brand while also spitting out content for 75 other brands that they don't bother to learn about or understand.

Most often, the person representing and posting for the brand has spent little time with the brand, and therefore lacks comprehensive knowledge and passion for the story. But hey, they put up posts, make some people LOL, and introduce some content. So what's the big deal?

Well, if they aren't educating and celebrating your story in partnership with the team, then the messaging isn't adding up, the brand isn't building relationships, and the content is wasting customer time—and that is a big deal.

Be careful of who takes the lead in your story celebration. Having a person or company guide your storytelling is a great strategy ... as long they possess the necessary tools, techniques, and strategies to make it succeed. Brand story execution requires the skillset, talent, and training of a specialist.

Even the smallest businesses now realize that social media execution is no longer something to have your part-time receptionist do on the side. If you have an internal team running the show, value that task enough to ensure that they are motivated, educated, and trained to get results.

Whoever is in charge of leading your social storytelling program has to be a passionate contributor and a leader who fully understands the brand story summary, the title, the storylines, and all of the reasoning behind those instruments. The quarterback(s) of your storytelling program needs to be aligned to steer the relationship from the inside out and the outside in. I cannot stress it enough:

> Whoever takes the leadership role for the program must be passionate and knowledgeable: know the company, know the industry, and function as a brand celebrator.

A decade ago, I intentionally built a high-relationship agency. I knew that you couldn't tell the story of a brand if you weren't committed to it. Every agency employee who represents the voice of a client's brand recognizes the responsibility to tell the story with pride and passion. Passionate brand celebrators know the brand, are passionate about the story, and are pumped up and excited to be a part of it. The quarterback of your program has to operate in this way. Period.

To generate trust and belief in your story, the brand must own the experience. Millions of other sources may be sharing different versions of your brand expectations, but you want to be the leading voice. Aim to make your brand stand above all others to lead the messaging. The best brands consistently reinforce their values through the celebration of their actions, input, and leadership.

Great companies start from internal education and grow that message every chance they get to maintain levels of trust and inspiration that their competitors can only hope to attain. When it comes to social sharing, you don't need to force-feed content or try to tell the story all at once. Educate one post at a time. Look at every social post as a little win. Make a plan to get to where you want to go and work your way there one post at a time. Do this, and the little wins will add up to make a big difference. When promoting your brand story in this manner, you aren't solely dependent on pay-per-click, a retail price, a promotion, or a single innovation. Success is driven by the strength of your story, the power of your title, and the stickiness of your storylines.

SUMMARY:

- Center your brand story celebration around content that harnesses the power of your brand story summary title and storylines.
- Powerful storylines stand out by expanding your reach, gaining enthusiasm, and building excitement.
- Subset ideas break the story into manageable content initiatives and set clear celebration expectations.

CHAPTER TEN

Starting the Celebration: Going from "Little i" to "Big I"

C HINESE PHILOSOPHER LAO TZU said, "He who knows others is wise. He who knows himself is enlightened." When team members absorb the brand story process, they relate to the message and see where they fit in. Creating a brand story celebration leads to this enlightenment.

It's an essential step because zealous team members want to see that the brand's story is authentic. They want to know how the story was uncovered, why it was written, and what it means. A brand story celebration facilitates this connection.

The clear brand story is presented and explained to the team members, and then the inspirational areas of the brand are brought to life through storylines. They help your team members to go deeper into the summary to dissect the story to see the specific roles they play in making it a reality.

TRANSFORMATIONAL CONNECTION

The aha moment occurs when a team member moves from seeing the story as a nonintegrated person to understanding the importance of their role in it. No longer on the outside, gauging interest and evaluating the message, they identify their role clearly. They understand how they contribute to the story and gain the ability to inspire and influence. This realization takes them from a "little i" individual to a "Big I" Influencer.

The brand story celebration educates individuals and advances their connection level by continually sharing content that brings the story to life. Through brand story participation, your team collectively illustrates to customers and employees that you don't just talk the talk, but you also walk the walk. The opportunity for a brand to provide this type of content is immense, but you have to have made it clear that your invitation encourages everyone, internally and externally, to participate, or the celebration won't happen.

GREATNESS BUILT FROM WITHIN

The key to starting a successful brand story celebration is being certain that you are introducing the brand story, title, and storylines in a manner that illustrates how the story was earned. The team needs to realize that this story separates their company from other brands. The message to the team is simply that the company is excited to educate as many people as possible on the story and storylines, and it would be awesome if they joined the celebration. Presenting the story in this way can be a catalyst in connecting your employees to what matters most: understanding, valuing, and delivering on the brand's promises. When management includes employees at this level, it increases education, motivation, and inspiration, and brings passion and energy to your business.

Oprah Winfrey said, "Passion is energy. Feel the power that comes from focusing on what excites you." If leaders want to make a long-term impact, focusing on bringing team members into the celebration from the start is best. When team members plug in and participate, they graduate from being disengaged individuals to being game-changing, story-building Influencers.

One of the best ways to be certain that your brand story celebration is fueled from within is to plan and execute a team roll-out meeting. Introduce the story, explain how it was earned, and review how team members can be a part of the plan to educate and inspire. It is a powerful way to get the party started.

The first time I presented a full brand story roll out presentation to a client's team was in a small conference room filled with 35 employees. I knew this team had been missing out on an appreciation of the company, their leader, and their story.

When I flew in to visit them a few months earlier, they were carefree and lax in their allegiance, with only a soft attachment to their company goals and an underappreciation for their owner. I learned the root of the disconnect weeks later when I executed a Brand Story assessment.

On a positive note, the Impression Analysis and survey revealed a company built on honesty, trust, and loyalty. The scores for the trust components were through the roof. As I mapped these connections, it became clear that the owner's character was the driving force that set the tone. His integrity, honesty, and loyalty formed the foundation of the company, but instead of celebrating that strength, a few bad apples were taking advantage of it. These team members led the charge in defining the owner's kindness as a weakness. They may not have been the majority, but the bad apples acted up, asserted themselves, and dominated as negative influencers.

The owner and other team members were so busy working and serving customers that they couldn't focus on correcting the culture. I was excited to display the assessment results to the team and felt this group was moments away from being enlightened. There was a lot to be proud of, and I couldn't wait to get the celebration started.

I began by reviewing the steps we took to uncover their brand story. I then unveiled and explained the brand story summary and title.

The presentation made a difference. I saw body language that indicated interest, but it wasn't unanimous. Nodding heads and smiles were scattered throughout the room, making it difficult to ascertain if the majority of the group connected with the message. That was about to change.

I stepped to the side and played their newly filmed brand story video on the projector screen. The three-minute depiction of their brand story allowed the inspiring aspects of their founder and the company to recognized, understood, and appreciated. It was an all-inclusive masterpiece.

I watched the team's faces as the story detailed how their honest approach and caring attitude was a driving force behind their business. Now, a larger group of heads were nodding and smiling in agreement. I saw pride in the company and in the owner as the video described the standards they were already living up to, how they build trust, and how they guarantee performance. Finally emotion set in as the story drove home the purposeful, unwavering goal for the company to do things right for their customers and the team.

Immediately after the video, the group erupted into an enthusiastic round of applause. Several people stood up to clap while others commented to the team members around them, and I noticed smiles around the room.

Watching the video, they saw their authentic brand story come to life. The story being unveiled set them up as spectators, being educated on how the company earned this reputation through the presentation of the brand story summary and title. Somehow, the video pulled it all together, celebrating the story in a manner that firmly connected all the dots. It brought the connection to life. The team was a part of something special, and now they knew it. Their enthusiasm still inspires me.

—

PEOPLE ARE ON A QUEST FOR AUTHENTICITY.
BUILDING A TRUE BRAND HELPS THEM
WITH THEIR QUEST.

—

Companies often underappreciate the benefits that enthusiasm brings to their brand development process. They see this eagerness as an outward display of an excited attitude. However, being enthusiastic is not just a mask—it comes from within. The word enthusiasm derives from the Greek word *enthousiasmos*, which means **inspiration**.

Sincere enthusiasm comes from the same authentic place as brand stories and is a natural connection. You cannot mandate or manufacture this type of experience, only inspire. When a brand educates with enthusiasm, the values and message of the story become clear and confident. It makes an impact.

Starting with this type of foundational support will lead people to connect and take part in the celebration of their brand story. Let's examine how to set up an education plan centered on building value and creating a path toward this kind of inspired brand participation.

From the president of a company to a cash register employee, few things are more powerful than pride in being a contributing member of a successful organization. It is exciting and rewarding to join in creating a memorable product, service, or experience. This transformational status of performance validates that you are doing things well, and it lets you know your actions are making a difference. That feeling has tremendous power because it transitions a person into an Influencer. It's a connection that motivates, inspires, and fuels participation in the celebration of the brand's story.

When team members understand their role in the execution of the brand story, it solidifies their place in the story. They feel pride in being a part of something bigger than themselves, and they can see beyond their role. Now their job is not solely about clocking in, clocking out, and getting by each day. They have a clear vision, enthusiastically making an impact: brand celebrators.

This heightened perspective is fueled by excitement, energy, and a sense of achievement. It inspires employees to contribute toward education, growth, and success by interjecting their insights and ideas into the story. Gaining team participation is a prerequisite to starting a brand story celebration—and the key to content development, connection, and brand success.

When leadership first presents a comprehensive brand story summary to a team, employees can see the brand as a whole to understand and appreciate the overall narrative. Whether done in person or recorded for an ongoing onboard presentation video, this first step is incredibly important. Explaining to the team allows each person to understand the process, and recognize and take pride in their hard-earned reputation.

The puzzle pieces join together and establish clarity in who the brand is and what it represents. However, there is a difference in the power gained from seeing everyone as a whole and the power gained from seeing your part in that story. When someone can clearly identify the way their input, assistance, and participation adds experiential value, it resonates on a distinct level. People want to make a difference, and when you can connect them to that opportunity, it is powerful. The clout of this type of connection extends beyond brand stories. In fact, if you look around, you can see examples of the power of meaningful association everywhere.

A CULINARY CONNECTION THAT MADE AN IMPACT

My mother is one of the hardest workers I have ever encountered. She got her Ed.D. from West Virginia University, and then worked long hours as a professor and Department Chair at Franciscan University. My father also earned his Ed.D. and was a school superintendent and university professor. Neither of my parents had much free time, but my mother still loved taking care of the house and her family. Her daily superwoman routine included preparing and serving every meal in our kitchen. She didn't have to do it, but it was a life that made her happy. The way she enjoyed working her way through the day was inspiring.

As my mother entered her 70s, she suffered a stroke and my do-it-all mother was in a battle. She fought like hell to regain control of her motor skills and made a full recovery. But at one point she was struggling to do her beloved daily activities, especially cooking.

I thought I might help by purchasing a few months of Blue Apron meals for her. The weekly Blue Apron kits included all of the ingredients with easy-to-follow recipes. My hope was that assembling and preparing the meals would be simple enough for her to execute with my father. The catch was that my dad didn't cook much, only occasionally participating in a one-man show outside on the grill. I never really witnessed him identifying a role that he could embrace in the kitchen, so I wasn't sure how it would go. The good news is that I got one hell of a surprise.

My dad went all in and embraced the opportunity. He saw the Blue Apron meals as a chance to get involved, work beside my mother, and help her through this difficult time. They were cooking meals, but it was something far more than that. They were working together, planning who would do what and using their own talents to create something together. For the first time, they were cooking dinner as a team. They FaceTimed me to display what they had cooked and exclaim how delicious it was. My mother was so happy to be cooking again, and my father was proud of his contribution. They worked together to make something greater. They made it a celebration, and the connection elevated the story way beyond "What's for dinner?"

LEADERSHIP NEEDS TO BE ONBOARD (A.K.A. CDM IS SIMPLE, NEVER EASY)

I was nervous that my father was not going to jump into a participatory role in the meal prep therapy idea. He had to connect the dots himself and be motivated in his own way for the idea to take off. Thankfully, he stepped up and bought in. My father has been a successful leader his whole life; however, the way he became a Celebrator for Blue Apron meals was special. Without his emphatic participation, the meal prep dishes would never have gotten made, the therapeutic experience for my mother would not have happened, and the celebration they shared would not have occurred. He connected to the most inspiring aspects, found his role in the story, and owned it.

As you can see by this example, even when the culture is just two people, leadership needs to connect with and embrace their role for a celebration to occur. When a leader fully supports the program and encourages participation from every person in the organization, the chances of the brand story message becoming ingrained into the culture multiplies dramatically.

Company leaders need to understand that marketing messages may sizzle, but brand stories bleed. They pump through the veins of the organizations. They live, they breathe, and they are real. When your story and storylines are revealed, every team member will take pride in the story because it is authentic and has been EARNED.

It is not about gimmicks or tricks. It's about the way your brand does business, how it works, and what it accomplishes.

It's a story worth telling, and everyone needs to be on board with spreading the message to as many supportive individuals as possible, using every channel imaginable. Let all team members know that telling the brand's story is not a task for the marketing team but an opportunity for all. Each person's participation is valuable because they all have the ability to influence and inspire. The goal is to spread the message, educate others, and help them understand why they would want to be part of the process. Clearly illustrate how they can contribute content, and when they do, celebrate their participation.

EVERYTHING IS WORKING?
KEEP FUELING IT

Celebrating your story takes commitment, patience, and perseverance. You cannot expect an army of supporters to jump on board immediately. It is difficult to put a timeline on educating, influencing, and inspiring others, as brand celebrations usually start small and build through a consistent and deliberate push to gain interest, support, and participation.

People bond on their own terms, and sometimes the journey to inspire a widespread celebration takes time. Charities, causes, and institutions are examples of organizations that stay committed to education, outreach, and targeted initiatives. They passionately promote their story and look for creative ways to extend their message, to build awareness, and to multiply their messaging. They remain patient, persistent and dedicated, looking for the right moment to push participation to bring their message into the spotlight.

In 2020, the Black Lives Matter movement became one of the greatest examples of what you can do when you believe that everyone has the ability to be an influencer. The movement exploded after George Floyd, a 46-year-old Black American man, was killed in Minneapolis, Minnesota, while in police custody. The incident was immediately followed by massive changes. New laws were put in place, enormous amounts of funding for Black Lives Matter projects poured in, and America began taking major steps toward progress that many had seen as impossible in the past. Statues came down, offensive brand images were removed, sports teams changed their names, and people all over the world began to loudly support the Black Lives Matter movement.

However, the power to generate this type of change through this campaign was not built overnight. The groundwork began in 2013 when Patrisse Cullors, Alicia Garza, and Opal Tometi founded Black Lives Matter. Now named the Black Lives Matter Global Network, it has over a dozen chapters and campaigns against violence and systemic racism toward Black people. Since its beginning, the movement has gained attention and participation. However, when George Floyd was killed in Minneapolis on May 25, 2020, the response was different. Gasoline had been pouring for decades, and George Floyd's murder became the match that ignited an inferno.

What allowed this to be a breakthrough moment for the Black Lives Matter movement were the commitment, passion, and persistence of those leading the charge. It wasn't one person, one action, or one illustration of injustice, but a culmination of the commitment to a story that needed to be celebrated. A story that educated others on the undeniable fact that racism is not only unacceptable; it is evil.

For many years prior to 2020, Black Lives Matter had passionately promoted education and awareness to gain support and participation using every opportunity available. The program grew through a long-term, sustained approach to education and support. When George Floyd's murder sparked outrage, the time was right. Black Lives Matter supporters were beyond ready to push these protests to the next level. This time they weren't going to settle for attention—they wanted action. They demanded that everyone become an influencer.

These passionate influencers took a hard-line approach and insisted that like-minded people speak up and get involved. If you believed that Black Lives Matter, your silence on this issue was unacceptable. The point of the movement and protest is that racial hate and bias make it necessary to celebrate that Black Lives Matter, and they need your help with that message.

The passionate push for participation made a difference, and the historic results continue, onboarding an army of unexpected influencers. Many teens and young adults in their twenties emerged as a powerful group of new activists. They saw social media beyond TikTok videos, DMs, and Instagram posts, realizing there was an opportunity to join in creating real change by using their platforms to spread education and awareness.

Black Lives Matter support surged to a whole new level. It gained backing all over the United States and from cities around the world. Individuals stood up and spoke out as influencers to celebrate the undeniable fact that Black Lives Matter. The protestors stood loud and proud, but were they actually "celebrators" of the #BlackLivesMatter story?

Without a doubt. The collective consciousness that fuels Black Lives Matter proponents to become influencers illustrates enthusiastic support for the movement. It is a celebration of a mindset. However, the celebration aspect of Black Lives Matter is often lost because, unfortunately, the call to action spawned outrage and incidents that were inconsistent with the true meaning and message. These actions are not what the movement is about, and the efforts of the people who get it wrong shouldn't be the focus.

The real story is the way enthusiastic individuals joined together to speak, dance, chant, and celebrate that story. The goal was to be heard, to inspire action, and to make a difference through a movement celebrated so prominently and dominantly that it overwhelms, influences, and inspires. The Black Lives Matter organizers pushed for participation, and it paid off because a strong celebration can't be ignored, especially when it is fueled with education, energy, and enthusiasm.

The Black Lives Matter movement pressed people to understand that "Yes, YOU are involved, and your role in this celebration is to step up, speak up and make your opinion known." As a result, an enormous amount of people realized their role and they spoke up on all sides. Tough conversations took place, and while controversy still exists, real change occurred.

It's tremendously inspiring when the manner of communication allows others to identify their role in the story personally. The feeling that you have a place in that story can be life-changing, because it pulls you in and activates your ability to influence.

> Joining in the celebration of a story means you're no longer going through the motions, but are taking part in collective consciousness through the celebration of a mentality and mindset.

Energy and involvement intensifies through enthusiasm, education, and interactions with other similar celebrators. You understand the story, you recognize your role, and your involvement intensifies. You emerge as an Influencer.

We've already reviewed the commitment, passion, and persistence it takes to connect in a way that fuels a brand celebration. Now let's look at some steps you can take to keep the celebration rolling on.

SUMMARY:

- The goal is to convert supporters from "little i" individuals to "Big I" Influencers.

- Make a plan to cultivate compatible team members from disengaged people to game-changing, story-building Influencers.

- Brand story roll-out meetings can make a big impact and solidify your celebration from the start.

- People want to make a difference, and when you can connect them to that opportunity, it is powerful.

- Leadership needs to connect with and embrace their role for a celebration to occur.

CHAPTER ELEVEN

The Frontline Fight

REMEMBER, THE ELEMENTS of a brand—the Attitude, Drive, and Direction—are required to create a Positive, Powerful, and Purposeful® organization. We can't have fakes, and Kendall Jenner won't be able to solve systemic racism by giving some police officer a Pepsi.

Storylines will engage us, and we've seen that leadership must be onboard to take advantage of opportunities. But all this work will be ruined unless key members of the team buy in, dig in, and begin to celebrate.

These unsung heroes of every company are your frontline workers who have customer encounters. The people that:

- Begin relationships
- Deliver your services
- Maintain relationships

Personnel in these roles have an opportunity and a responsibility to advance your story. When they are armed with the story, they can access mentors who know and teach the story, and be surrounded by reminders and tools that perpetually reinforce the culture. Support for celebrating your brand's story isn't a hard sell. Salespeople, company leadership, and frontline employees all benefit immensely from a strong brand story celebration.

IT STARTS WITH SALESPEOPLE: THE ONES WHO OPEN A RELATIONSHIP

When a salesperson is trying to educate someone—rather than manipulating them—they reinforce the real live, best parts of your brand. They drive your culture forward and set the tone for the relationship you want with the clients you want, who will help you form the business you want.

Cultural Development Marketing gives salespeople more opportunities than any other employee because they have the most to gain: a chance to compete for business with something other than a discount. That makes it a lot easier to begin a relationship with a new customer.

When presenting an offer, they provide something better than your competitors. They exhibit your whole company, your values, and the honest differences between companies. Spectators will become interested, and interested people share the fact that they worked with your company because of your values, not price.

How many times have you heard a friend bragging about their new purchase? "Well, it cost a little more at this company, but it's truly worth it." Probably often, and living up to the story you've discovered is the way that you create, sustain, and maintain that opportunity.

Mercedes, Tiffany's, Starbucks, Apple, Louis Vuitton, and Disneyland all charge more than their competitors … and they all have raving fans and tons of brand value.

LEADERS MUST MAINTAIN A CULTURE OF COMMITMENT AND INTEGRITY

Personnel who interact with customers have to be committed to advancing your storylines. From the person who first answers the phone to the support rep who solves a problem after the sale, each employee is part of the story.

It's not enough to talk about it. You have to be about it, especially internally. The things you say and do have to matter to you, and you have to mean what you say. If a leader isn't committed, it will spread like cancer.

- The frontline employees won't be committed,
- The sales team won't be committed, and
- That will damage the brand.

Imagine what would happen if:

- Your brand story is about integrity but a salesperson takes an ethical shortcut, OR
- You promise friendly service but your phone is answered rudely, OR
- You promise expertise but your technician doesn't know what he's working on.

The company needs to be who they "post" to be. If your actions contradict the promises of your story, the narrative is a hoax. The situation will be worse because you've made—and broken—a promise.

You have to stay committed to celebrating the true meaning behind your brand story, presenting authentic examples, and backing up your brand promise.

Don't fake it. Feel it.

Don't say it. Show it.

Don't promise it. Prove it.

CREATING A SYSTEM TO CELEBRATE

We have already discussed the importance of creating a content plan to celebrate your story using media channels. However, brands must also remember to create a content plan for the frontline team members who have a chance to educate your customers face to face. To make the most of every exchange, these team members need resources and structure.

The goal is to help your sales team share your story in the most effective way possible. Take the time to develop innovative ideas and create materials that systemize the presentation of your brand's story. The goal is to provide guidance and assistance without impacting their individuality and freedom. You don't want robots out in the field, but you can increase your team's ability to informally educate with the right tools.

Brands can also create programs, processes, and technology that sets the brand up for ongoing story celebration success. There are many new and innovative options that can be used to educate while adding excitement and generating interest. However, brands will also find that their newly defined brand story summary, title, and storylines will breathe new life into many of the tools and techniques they have used in the past. Once the brand story is clear, options for educating and celebrating open up.

THE RELATIONSHIP AGREEMENT

Outlined relationship agreements in some form or fashion exist in almost any industry. I have seen these agreements referred to as partnership plans, VIP programs, and more. I consistently refer to these types of instruments as relationship agreements because I think the relationship aspect is what matters most. Whatever you call them, they are perfect tools to align with the process of Culture Development Marketing.

By definition, relationship agreements create an opportunity to outline and educate others on the value of a relationship with the brand. However, many brands are short-sighted in the way they execute the messaging and delivery of these agreements.

The biggest mistake that brands make is to exclusively use these agreements to illustrate how customers can personally benefit from the brand. It is important to detail consumer value by explaining how customers can gain discounts, receive incremental add-ons or benefit from special services. However, your relationship agreement can do much more for your customers and your culture.

Relationship agreements should also be used to share the most inspiring aspects of your organization's story in a repeatable, trainable format.

Companies who know their clear brand story have the ability to use this agreement as a way to educate customers on who they are and what they are all about. The goal is to find ways to creatively and pridefully celebrate your history, culture, founder's story, core values, unique systems, and much more.

Each idea becomes a talking point for your frontline team members to use in educating the customer 1-on-1. Leadership should prioritize the presentation of the agreement, train on it, and make sure that EVERY team member who has the ability to share this agreement embraces the opportunity.

When you create a systemized approach to presenting your relationship agreements in this way, this tool will not only strengthen relationships with the customer but also reinforce the values and attributes to the presenting team member.

Prioritizing the presentation in this way is a shift that transitions the agreement from a sales tool to a relationship builder.

If you aren't utilizing your relationship agreements in this way, you are missing a tremendous CDM opportunity to build your culture and relationships simultaneously with your team and clients/customers.

ENHANCED LOYALTY EXPERIENCES FULFILL BRAND PROMISES

Loyalty programs are another tool that has been around for decades. However, today, brands are taking loyalty programs to a different level by creating educational interactive experiences, delivering bonuses, sharing information, and more. One way to differentiate and educate through a rewards program is to include unique ideas related to the brand.

For example, the Pittsburgh Pirates offer the opportunity to throw out a first pitch or take part in a session of batting practice as perks in packages for their most loyal sponsors. This experiential marketing opportunity only costs them time and coordination, but the benefactor's experience is priceless, memorable, and interactive. It results in an exciting and memorable participatory relationship. Who can forget the thrill of throwing a first pitch on a professional baseball field or stepping on a professional field to take a few whacks at a ball?

The best loyalty programs are less about saying "We give you this" and more about "We're here for you." Developing loyalty programs to illustrate the relationship's value is a bigger opportunity. When you broaden your perspective, include immersive ideas, and embrace the opportunity to use your program to advance a connected person from Spectator to Appreciator to Celebrator, you cement brand story education and celebration into your culture.

Design a loyalty program with the frontline employees in mind. Even if you use an app to manage your loyalty program, let it reinforce the brand standards and reference the customer opportunities.

EVEN AN APP CAN ACT AS AN INFLUENCER

Starbucks does a phenomenal job of doing more and going further with their app, which is a Brand Celebrator conversion machine. Sure, the users of the Starbucks app are able to work their way to free cups of coffee through goals set in the Starbucks Rewards program, but the app does more. It's a communications portal that educates, builds value, and inspires participation.

Notifications pop up, reminding users to stop by. They inform you of daily specials, and even send you a birthday gift. Starbucks customers can use the app to order ahead, like a VIP, so their coffee will be waiting for them on the counter. The app remembers their preferences, keeps a history of their purchases, and gives them personalized offers. A message inbox teaches them about new menu items. They learn all about the features, from the calories and ingredients contained in their Roasted Pepper Egg White Bites to the intricacies of the Sous Vide cooking style they use to prepare them. Through the app, a person participates and learns, and the relationship grows.

Starbucks knows that most customers won't visit their website to read about their products, their service, and their culture. Instead, the app takes a forward, inclusive approach to onboarding celebrators by systematically providing content and finding ways to educate customers in a trusting manner. Education and inspiration surround the Starbucks brand because they have a content plan that creates a concerted effort to inspire and educate through what they do. From their app to their in-store experiences to their social media postings, they have a process for building brand celebrators.

HOW THE "BIG GUYS" GAIN LOYALTY AND INFLUENCE

Some of the most successful brands of our time have excellent processes for advancing relationships.

- **Amazon Prime:** Amazon built their Prime Membership as a way to celebrate their innovative attitude and their commitment to providing game-changing value, pushing the boundaries to upgrade the value and experience. The idea turned heads in the online shopping world upside down, from offering Prime members free two-day shipping to free one-day shipping to free same-day shipping to the current free two-hour delivery in some markets. However, Prime Membership is far more than free shipping. Free Amazon Video and exclusive customer perks and benefits educate customers on the Amazon items and services that enhance lives. A sense of community and celebration are forged through participation events, like Amazon Prime Day. In creating a company culture centered on more than just price, Amazon successfully uses its Prime Membership to build relationships, gain influence, and get personal.

- **Grammarly:** Computers have checked our spelling and grammar for years, and while the basic feature is useful, it never stood out, and no one recognized it was an area where a relationship hole existed. Grammarly stepped into the scene and created a personalized relationship through a suite of services centered on helping people communicate more effectively. The company has experienced tremendous success because it sets itself up as more than a valuable writing tool: it establishes a motivational relationship with the writer. In addition to the functionality of the app, Grammarly shares valuable information on their blog that helps readers write better, reach their audience, and be successful in business and life. The company culture is solidified by letting you know how much they care about your success. A system is in place for personalized communication with Grammarly users through email updates that spotlight a user's participation. A weekly score is presented for comparison, and they also show you how much your writing is improving. They celebrate participation, keep users in the know, and make the act of grading your writing feel like a supportive process.

- **Pandora:** Pandora, a music platform, builds personal relationships based on participation. The company's mission statement is "To play only music you'll love." They live that assertion by building a unique reciprocal relationship where they can create shared value through education and participation. Pandora learns from their listeners when they "Thumbs Up" or "Thumbs

Down" a song. The users then learn from Pandora because the company uses their participation data not to only present the songs the user told them they loved, but also to introduce similar songs and artists. In August 2020, Pandora's website reported they were providing their highly personalized listening experience to approximately 70 million patrons each month. Users manage the platform through a mobile app, the internet, and integrations with over 2,000 connected products. That's a seriously involved relationship, which Pandora extends in the way they market and communicate to listeners. For example, they send updates congratulating listeners on how many songs they gave a Thumbs Up to and how long they listened. They are an ultimate celebration brand because it's hard for listeners to avoid the undeniable idea that the more they participate, the better Pandora will provide the music they love.

- **Dollar Shave Club:** It's not a surprise that a successful company with the word "club" in their name would excel in building celebratory relationships. The mail-order shave club burst on the scene with a memorable brand story video that educated men on a new way to stock shaving supplies. The invitation to participate in the story is direct, as the company isn't trying to build customer relationships: they want members. To them, these associates matter most. The owner, the employees, and the customers are all members. That's a significant distinction from the start. Their website builds a relationship with you immediately by walking you through a survey of your preferences and needs, showing they value your time and want to be targeted and relevant in their products and information offers. They also use their mail-order approach to continuously educate and build their relationship with members by taking a cool, minimalistic approach in their messaging. It doesn't seem like they are selling as much as they are educating and advising members. They are building more than a persona with their brand; they are solidifying their company culture, staying true to the brand through marketing that has an inclusive personality. It feels like it's a true club.

LEADERS NEED REAL INTEGRITY, NOT RAH-RAH SPEECHES

Leadership needs a plan for success when it comes to executing CDM. The level of emphasis that leadership puts on celebrating the story has a big impact on CDM's success. Every leader needs to be behind the brand promises and put processes in place to ensure success.

ONBOARDING

Creating an onboarding system is a necessary step in assuring the long-term success of your company's brand story celebration. As businesses grow, a primary point that strains the quality of culture and connection is onboarding. Welcoming team members, telling them what they need to know, and making sure they're on the same page can be challenging for small companies—and nearly impossible for larger companies. The key is to design a foundation of content that educates new team members systematically on the brand's story, your core values, the programs that matter most, and the ideas that shape the experience.

TRAINING

Tools only work when the person using them knows what they are for and how to use them. Your brand story education tools are no different. Leadership needs to make sure that there is mandatory training for any brand story celebration tools that need it. The brand's ability to educate using these tools increases exponentially when team members are clear on optimal usage. When you put in a system that lets team members know the best way to present your relationship agreement, how to use your company content sharing app, or the proper way to present the company's signature loyalty program, everybody wins.

CULTURE CARDS

A culture card is a dedicated card that can fit in employee wallets or be tucked into their monitors to remind them of the story. All kinds of company cards have been created to reinforce mission statements, promote goals, affirm a mindset, or serve as a reminder for a key process. One company even produced a steel card for the team members who demonstrated the top five attributes in the Impression Analysis. The key is to make the card meaningful and memorable.

The Ritz-Carlton famously initiated a "Credo Card" to proudly celebrate and reinforce the expectations of the Ritz-Carton story. The card covers all the bases, featuring:

- Their credo (similar to a brand story)
- Their motto (like a brand story title)
- And their three steps of service, employee promise, and service values (supporting storylines)

Through the card, Ritz-Carlton sets up a celebration of the attitude of their team, how they operate, and the outcomes they seek to deliver. The card was given to every team member, helping automate the practice of celebrating the story's values on an ongoing basis.

INTERNAL SIGNAGE

Internal signage displays brand story tags that demonstrate values and provide a gentle, ambient reminder of how good your team is. Create the layout of your HQ to emphasize your brand in the board room, on the building, in the office area, warehouse, break room, or anywhere that makes a statement and helps employees understand the message and its importance. The right signage support plan can help reinforce your values and promote participation, while serving as a constant reminder of the expectations associated with the brand story.

BRAND STORY FILMS

Short of face-to-face communication, there is no better way to share knowledge and education than by video. For that reason, more and more companies have been creating brand story films. A short video about your brand and the reasons behind your choices can reinforce the brand and help visual learners really connect with it. Over the past decade, our team has worked to perfect a process of celebrating brand stories and storylines through engaging and authentic films. These films should not be designed as promotional material with a short shelf life. They are long-term educational instruments that shape your culture by reinforcing values, sharing your beliefs, and building relationships.

When done correctly, and as a reflection of reality, these films are compelling and can set the tone for future brand celebrations.

REMEMBER: YOUR FRONT LINE STARTS INSIDE YOUR WALLS

As you roll out CDM, you have to win the war internally before you can extend it externally. If your internal team won't share in the celebration, you have zero chance of creating a celebration, whether internal or external.

You have to influence your team before that influence can spread. Far too often, leaders want to take shortcuts and not invest in the messaging, time, and materials it takes to make this work. Those shortcuts make it harder for them to spread their message or take advantage of the unbelievable opportunities that exist to communicate and celebrate. Make sure that you take the time to plan for the initial and ongoing success of your brand story celebration.

SUMMARY:

- Everyone in your company has an opportunity and a responsibility to advance your story.

- The right tools are required to help your team celebrate in the most meaningful way.

- Loyalty programs and relationship agreements can be critical components to building long-term relationships inside and outside the company.

- Get creative: Build programs and partnerships around who you are.

- Find ways to highlight the unique aspects of your brand and how they deliver the greatest value.

CHAPTER TWELVE

All In to Win

I GREW UP WHERE the Pittsburgh Pirates baseball franchise enjoyed a lot of success as one of the major franchises that made Pittsburgh the "City of Champions" back in the 1970s and '80s. They were my favorite baseball team.

When I moved to Bradenton, Florida, 17 years ago, it seemed like destiny that the town had been the Pittsburgh Pirates spring training home since 1969. That feeling got stronger when I secured a relationship for my company to provide a variety of marketing services for the Pittsburgh Pirates and their minor league team, the Bradenton Marauders. One of the greatest joys of my career is having the opportunity to work with the Pittsburgh Pirates for over a decade now.

It is an amazing honor to call them my client. Cheering them on throughout my life and working for the Pirates has been a wild ride. They were successful when I was growing up, and even won a World Series Championship when I was a kid. However, when we began working together in 2009, the team hadn't experienced a winning season since 1992. It has not been an easy road for Pirates fans. Ownership had changed hands a few times, and a line of managers had come and gone. After many disappointments, Pirates fans were beginning to lose hope.

Things changed when the Pirates hired manager Clint Hurdle in 2010. Having recently led the Colorado Rockies to their first National League pennant and World Series Championship series, Hurdle was a hot commodity in the coaching world. He had plenty of opportunities to coach in more prolific markets, so why come to Pittsburgh?

He told *Baseball Weekly* that it came down to one question that he asked of the Pirates' General Manager Neal Huntington and President Frank Coonelly. "I looked them in the eye and asked, 'Are you all in?'" recalled Hurdle. "And they said, '[We're] in.'"

"Are You All In?" became Hurdle's calling card. He started inside with the owners, then educated the players and entire organization on what it meant to be "All In," and how to become known for that mentality. He made certain that those inside the organization knew that living a commitment to the "All In" story wasn't about honoring a slogan—it was about contributing to the culture.

Hurdle led the commitment to change, got initial buy-in from the front office, onboarded his players, and then looked to develop it through their fans. He extended his "Are You All In?" challenge beyond the organization, and the motivational inquiry created a viral buzz online and in the media. The media connected with the message and began asking Pirates fans, "Are YOU in ... like Clint?" It was a perfect example of a story impacting an organization so dramatically from the inside out that it was able to generate enough inspiration to bring people in from the outside.

In just one year, his leadership and passion made an impact. At the 2011 All-Star break, the Pirates had a 47–43 record and were one game out of first place in their division. It was the first time the Pirates had been over .500 going into the All-Star break in almost 20 years. They finished with 15 more wins than they had in 2010. The best news of all was that fan confidence and morale were renewed.

Leading into the 2012 season, I remember attending a pre-season Spring Training season ticket–holder event. The crowd of 1,000 Pirates fans included my parents, three-decade Pirates season ticket holders. They were sitting at my table when Coach Hurdle stopped by, sat down, and asked if he could sit with us until he had to speak. He talked to my mom, made jokes with my dad, and then shook everyone's hand as he rose to take the stage. Kind acts like this happen routinely for Hurdle, and they give you an idea of his amazing character and personality.

He walked up to the stage and addressed the fans in his usual inspiring way, and then asked if anyone had questions. I'll never forget the first question, or his answer. A gruff man who was sitting right in front of the stage asked, "What are your goals for this season?" Coach Hurdle paused and then confidently said, "We have the same goal every year. That goal is to win a World Championship. But we can't just say that we want that to happen. We have to commit to the actions and attitude needed to get it done." He finished by saying, "I tell the guys every day that vision without action and attitude is just an illusion. You need all three to be all in."

In other words, you can't just set your sights on success. You have to back it up with what you do and the way you do it. This relates directly to the importance of a complete story that includes Attitude, Drive, and Direction.

I can't say that I was surprised by his statement. From the start, Hurdle focused on developing a story of success within the organization. That story was built upon what he believed to be the necessary ingredients to success: vision, action, and attitude.

He stressed the importance of taking part in the celebration of the story by asking others to join him in going all in. Through his confident leadership, he inspired the Pirates to live, breathe, and celebrate their story.

After their amazing 2011 rebound season, Hurdle and the team promised that they would improve, finish strong, and stay committed to being all in. That is exactly what they did. Although the playoffs eluded them in 2012, their record improved and progress was made.

In 2013, after 21 straight losing seasons, the Pirates produced a winning season and made the playoffs for the first time since 1992. Their success made them the most surprising team in baseball, and it also made their lead Brand Celebrator, Clint Hurdle, Major League Baseball's 2013 Manager of the Year. The success continued in 2014 as the team once again improved their record, made the playoffs, and Clint Hurdle was selected as a finalist for Major League Baseball's Coach of the Year for the second year in a row.

Coach Hurdle made the playoffs once more during his career with the Pirates, and although his time in Pittsburgh ended without winning a World Series Championship, he made his mark in history by steadily returning winning baseball to Pittsburgh after two decades of losing seasons. He changed the narrative with an "Are You All In?" mentality that brought excitement and energy back to Pittsburgh Pirates baseball.

I was all in as an inspired Celebrator, and the experience was awesome. The influence that Clint Hurdle was able to produce in such a short time showed how much impact a person with the right mindset can make. His enthusiasm and confidence literally willed a brand story celebration into existence. I have seen many examples of this over the years, but this is one of my favorites.

Unfortunately, I have also seen a great deal of instances where the attitude and influence of leadership missed the mark, and literally put an end to the party.

CONFIDENCE IS A CRITICAL INGREDIENT

Once when I spoke at a leadership event, a business owner was visibly connected with my discussion about the importance of celebrating your story. He was all the way in the back of the room, but he was feverishly jotting down notes, nodding in agreement, and focusing on the content. The moment I finished speaking, he rushed up and began telling me that he needed me to help his business. He said that CDM "was exactly what [his] business needed."

He explained that he owned midsized appliance stores and needed help telling his story. For decades, his success in the appliance business came through an emphasis on having the lowest prices. However, the business had changed, and bigger competitors had changed the game. Big-box stores like Lowes, Home Depot, and Best Buy surrounded him, and their marketing strategy was geared toward being the low-price leader. He was confident that it was only a matter of time before his low-cost reputation would erode to a level that his business could not be sustained.

He saw Culture Development Marketing as a way to differentiate his business from those big-box brands. His eagerness inspired me, so I agreed to meet him the next week at his store.

It was clean, well-lit, and modern. More importantly, there was great character in their service, uniqueness in their systems, and strength through the quality of people on the team. They certainly seemed functional, and they appeared to have a compelling story to tell.

We began the process, and I felt confident that we could uncover a story that they would be proud to celebrate. I was onboard.

The Impression Analysis quickly showed that the story was even more compelling than I anticipated. The top five impressions were reputable, knowledgeable, community oriented, family oriented, and local. Their business was, in fact, a lot more than just price. As we dug deeper, it was clear that the most inspiring impressions were happening due to their processes and their people. Customers had immense appreciation for the unique steps they took to deliver caring service. There was also a storyline emerging through the innovative way they cultivated contractor partnerships. It became clear that this was a personality-driven sales process.

Once I had the Impression Analysis results in mind, the summary seemed to pull itself together. I formalized the results and presented the findings to the owner and the management team. They loved the summary. It was clear, eye-opening, and on target. It shone a light on who they were as a team, what they meant to the community, and how they delivered value through their products. It was comprehensive, and it was inspiring. They were ready to roll with it.

We ended the meeting discussing the next steps and roughly creating a timeline for finalizing a content plan, shooting a brand story video, and rolling out the program to the rest of the team. I stressed the importance of being fired up about the program to create contagious enthusiasm. We wanted to get the entire team on board as brand celebrators. Everyone agreed. I left the meeting shaking hands and seeing smiles, with all of them assuring me they were ready. However, something changed overnight.

The owner called the next day with questions. He said that he kept looking at the Impression Analysis results and wanted to discuss the importance of "competitive" being seen as his #9 impression. He saw opportunity, even after acknowledging that it wasn't a top perception. He thought that if he pushed price and competitiveness a little more, maybe it would deliver the results that his competitive pricing strategy had achieved in the past. I quickly asked him how much of his marketing over the past year was devoted to price. "100 percent," he said. I smiled at his quick answer and said, "How much more can you push something past 100 percent?"

He had been driving competitive pricing as hard as he could, and admitted it was not working. That failing strategy is what encouraged him to ask about uncovering his story in the first place.

As he opened up more, his reliance on price came out in full force. The chances for success in rolling out the program were not looking good. However, I didn't panic. Instead, I once again presented the Impression Analysis. I demonstrated that competitiveness had a place in the story, just not the starring role. The inspiring aspects of his brand were far more beneficial to helping him build relationships—especially since he had been losing the price game.

I had no interest in "selling him" on the validity of his uncovered story, or the importance of leading with his strengths in story development. I was trying to reconnect the path to his original mindset because, without his support, the program couldn't work. I also wasn't there to beg him to onboard his team—it would never work that way. You can't construct a culture of brand story celebration with hesitancy. You have to do it with confidence, and if you want to inspire a brand celebration, you have to buy in and believe.

Our process uncovered a solid understanding of his brand's story, and I recognized the most inspiring aspects of his brand. I saw how they would connect: the story was ready to go. But he wasn't. He could not get past his fear of change.

He couldn't help himself. The pressures of his business had intensified the need to succeed quickly. That feeling multiplied the allure of quick reward, price-point marketing, and it was crushing his ability to create change with his story. The opportunity was there, but he could not embrace it. As much as I would have loved to be a part of telling his story and generating brand celebrators for his business, it simply could not be done without leadership support, positive energy, and confidence. The leader of the company needs to be proud of the story and eager to begin celebrating it; otherwise, it will never work.

—

ANYONE CAN CUT PRICES.
IT TAKES COMMITMENT TO CELEBRATE STORIES.

—

The fact is that anyone can compete with products and services for a price. The true measure of differentiation is the experience your brand delivers through its people. Ultimately, your brand is only as strong as the harmony that exists between the story you tell and the way it is being lived.

Generating support and enthusiasm for your newly defined brand story is a process centered on the idea of relationship advancement, one step at a time: First from inside out, and then from the outside in. Many companies want to speed up the process, and some want it to happen overnight. Leaders need to realize that CDM requires a confident, long-term commitment.

WHAT HAPPENS WHEN YOU DON'T COMMIT ...

Even with commitment, you might not win every time. But if you don't commit, you guarantee you won't win.

The approach of the appliance retailer we highlighted and the approach of Clint Hurdle are vastly different, but the main difference is the mindset. You need to be motivated to start a celebration because it begins with you. Gaining support or building brand participation won't happen without your excitement to lead the charge.

It does not make sense to uncover a brand story if you don't get behind a full-blown celebration. It's like having a Ferrari but never turning it on, taking it for a ride, and feeling the exhilaration from its performance. You are not merely introducing a story, but firing up your engine of influence, hitting the gas, and living your story to its full potential. That is how you generate pride, excitement, and support for the story, its meaning, and what it represents. Fueling this type of inspiration is the goal of CDM.

Every person in your organization must comprehend that this is more than a marketing message—it represents who the brand is, how it functions, and the experience it delivers. Presenting your brand story summary is not the same as reciting your "unique selling proposition" or asking employees to memorize your mission statement.

Present a comprehensive story that highlights the most inspiring aspects of the brand. It is a different approach where you passionately develop your culture around a core brand story that sets up expectations, celebrates who you are, and inspires participation.

That type of connection doesn't just transform a team member into a Brand Celebrator, but it also makes them great at what they do.

Stanford professor and well-respected business researcher Jim Collins may have said it best when assessing the participation style of the top leaders he has examined in his 25 years of work in the field. "The great leaders I've studied are all people whose energy and drive are directed outward. It's not about themselves. It's about something greater." As Collins points out, people are able to function with inspired excellence when they go beyond themselves to understand and connect with the bigger story.

Creating your brand story celebration begins with your team. These are the brand celebrators who represent your brand each day. They face the world as your front line—and they experience thousands of opportunities to connect your organization to the world at large.

Building an organization of brand celebrators generates greater engagement and loyalty among existing customers, a reputation that will act as a magnet for both talent and new customers, and finally, peak performance for your organization. If team members aren't excited or don't seem to care about a common goal, what happens to the brand experience? Nothing good. On the other hand, when a committed, enthusiastic team initiates a ripple effect of enthusiasm through their Positive Attitude, Powerful Drive, and Purposeful Direction, people take notice. They want to be a part of the excitement.

Leading your brand story celebration with enthusiasm affords the power to influence and inspire, but the leadership has to be all in to make it work. The best leaders function as lead celebrators who lead the charge. They clearly and confidently connect with similar employees to lead them to be excited about the work they do, to be happier as part of a team, and to become more fulfilled in their life.

"A good leader inspires people to have confidence in the leader; a great leader inspires people to have confidence in themselves."

~ ELEANOR ROOSEVELT

You cannot cautiously step halfway into being an inspiring leader. When deciding to pursue a goal of any size or importance, commit and devote yourself to that endeavor. Whether it's getting ready to speak in front of a group, taking part in a competition, or looking to develop brand celebrators, too much caution kills confidence and will crush your performance.

YOUR ATTITUDE (GOOD OR BAD) IS HIGHLY CONTAGIOUS

When a leader doesn't commit, it won't spread in the organization. But stories and success can happen when any key team member commits. If you decide to step up and lead in any situation, acknowledge the obstacles that stand in your way, take ownership of them, believe in yourself, and go for it.

A few years ago, my wife Samantha and I took our family to Tennessee to stay at a friend's cabin in the hills of Pigeon Forge, overlooking a river. Our first time experiencing the beauty of this amazing location, the Smoky Mountains, blew us away. The house sits above a bend in the Little Pigeon River called "Shinbone," where a cliff rises 25 feet above a deep pool of water.

The river was beautiful, but I wasn't interested in diving in—I was getting too old for that kind of adventure. My boys were 8, 11, and 13. They were not known for being daredevils, so I didn't think that they'd want to jump off the cliff. I felt certain they would be 100 percent against it. We were told stories of people who had been coming to Shinbone for decades to jump off that cliff, but we weren't interested.

On day three of our vacation, we decided to take a walk along the river. As we came back, we passed a neighbor cutting his grass. He looked at us and yelled over the noise of the mower, "Have y'all jumped off Shinbone yet?" I yelled back, "No, not yet," and kept walking. But he wouldn't let me go.

He turned off the mower, walked over to us, and said, "What do you mean you haven't done it?! It's right there!" I told him that I wasn't even sure where the jumping point was on the cliff. He came closer and said, "Every person I know has jumped off that cliff, and not a one of them has done anything but had fun." He continued talking as he walked past. "I'll show you where the jump point is, but I can already tell that you won't do it."

As we all followed him to the cliff's edge just 30 yards from where we first spoke, he stood on the jumping point. "This is it." At that time, in front of my three boys, I began to consider jumping. I stepped up to a few feet from the edge and said, "You know what? I think I can do this."

The problem was that I "considered" and "thought about" if I could do it. But I didn't believe it, and I certainly didn't want to do it. As I took off my shoes and stepped up to the edge, I looked down and tried to work up the courage to jump. If you have ever hesitantly approached the edge of a swimming pool diving board as a kid, you know the "Oh boy, this is too high!" feeling.

As I hesitated, I heard my eight-year-old son Koby barking at me. "Dad, I can do it! Dad, let me do it! Dad, I want to jump!" Exaggeration was not uncommon for Koby, so I didn't think he was serious. I shushed him and explained that I needed to focus.

As my boys sat quietly and my new grass-cutting friend watched, I gave up. I stepped back from the edge and laughingly said, "I think I just need to think about this for a second."

The man tried to let me off the hook. "I know, it looks high when you're standing there getting ready to jump." His consolation only added to my embarrassment.

I stood there awkwardly, trying to motivate myself to jump. Koby started back up: "Dad, I'll do it. Please let me do it. Dad, Dad, Dad ..." I was trying to focus and knew he wouldn't jump, so I looked at him and said, "Yeah, Koby, sure. Go ahead and ..." That's all I got out before his little feet scurried over the edge and he went airborne.

My other two boys looked at me with their mouths wide open. I was in complete shock as well. I was scared to look down to see where he was, but as we all did so, he popped up to the surface. He was smiling and shouted, "That was awesome!" The grass-cutting neighbor was happy to rub it in my face. "Now that's how you do it!"

My middle son Kyle immediately took off his shirt. "If Koby did it, I'm doing it!" In an instant, he launched himself off the cliff. The two laughed together below as my oldest son Kelly Jr. looked at me and said, "Dad, I'll only go if you go." I still didn't want to jump, but now I had to.

I stepped up and jumped, and so did Kelly Jr. We all overcame an obstacle, and we celebrated together. I did it a few more times, and the boys jumped dozens of times during our remaining three days of vacation.

The lesson I learned from standing on that cliff is, *If you are going to do something, you have to have confidence in yourself and be willing to commit to doing what you need to do.*

If you are busy weighing your options and fail to make a commitment, you set yourself up for failure. Standing on that edge and looking down at the water, I spent too much time analyzing the situation and letting fear take over. I should have just jumped.

I had already assessed the situation before I stepped up to the edge. I was confident that it was safe, and I knew it was something I could do. But I allowed my fears and doubts to restrict my actions. That day, the leaders who stepped up to encourage and inspire me were my sons, and I was the one who followed them.

A fearless attitude is not necessarily good, nor is approaching your business recklessly. Assess the situation ahead of time and make an educated decision. However, when you decide that you are ready, you need to go at it 100 percent. More sports injuries are caused during low-contact practices than actual games because people just can't naturally "turn it on and off."

—

FEARLESSNESS ISN'T RECKLESSNESS.

—

In the face of change, you will find a friend in fear if you look for it, but that's the easy way out. It takes courage to push yourself toward meaningful action. People get lost in a continual cycle of mulling over each option within each decision for so long that they become completely overwhelmed by all of the potential possibilities. They freeze in a state of panicked indecision, unable to take even the simplest actions. I describe this as a nasty case of "Analysis Paralysis."

You cannot be a leader in developing brand celebrators throughout your organization while being strangled by obstacles. They are the natural combatants to connecting with a Positive Attitude, Powerful Drive, and a Purposeful Direction.

- Fear restricts your emotions and passion, and affects your Attitude.

- Doubts influence Drive, corrupting strength, confidence, and commitment.

- Limiting beliefs impede Direction, infecting your vision and purpose.

We unintentionally beat ourselves down with negativity, impede our progress, and stand in the way of connection. The owner of the appliance store succumbed to his negative feelings, and it cost him the opportunity to experience a whole new level of success with his company and team. He is not alone. We all deal with obstacles in life. However, it is possible to develop a plan to rise above constricting emotions.

Success and self-confidence happen when you can walk through these feelings and direct your thoughts and actions. Even though it is difficult, each time we exercise our right to be bigger than these emotions, we build our self-confidence and increase our chances for success. Understanding this unlocks the opportunity to be an influencer at any level you choose.

SUMMARY:

- A single inspired Celebrator can make an enormous impact, leading the charge in a brand's celebration.

- Confidence is critical: You cannot step halfway to success.

- If you don't commit, you guarantee you won't win.

- Avoid Analysis Paralysis: When you decide to go, jump in.

Celebrate. Educate. Dominate.

ONTENT CREATION, HIGHLIGHTING and promoting your uniqueness isn't "extra" these days. It's now mandatory. Every business is vulnerable to disruption from established competitors, giant companies, and now even "apps" like Handy or Uber.

Leadership and HR departments can no longer sit back and allow team members to sit in the role of spectators. Not only does this oversight impair their team's performance; they also risk losing key individuals who find it challenging to grow their connection. Leadership needs to make sure that their content plan and brand celebration are centered around advancing the relationships from Spectator to Appreciator to Celebrator.

When organizations keep these stages top-of-mind, they can easily assess each position and look for opportunities to advance relationships.

- Spectators can see the story, but they aren't necessarily motivated or excited by it. They show up to work, but they have yet to make a personal connection to their role in the story. Their attitude, effort, and results are uninspired.

- Appreciators understand their role. They are aware of the value that the company brings to their life and recognize the relevance and importance of their work. They get the job done, but they may not be excited about the company as a whole.

- Celebrators are enthusiastic about the company and their work. They believe in the organization, and they care about its future. Their support and participation become a valuable source of growth, inspiration, and influence.

Keep the advancement of these relationships a priority. Your culture cannot remain stagnant, allowing team members to sit in a spectator state. Assess your team's involvement and appreciation level on a continual basis.

Do your team members …

- Realize that their work is meaningful?
- Feel recognized and appreciated for their work?
- Receive support in a way that makes them feel like they fit in?
- Feel encouraged to share ideas and experiences?

To develop a rich, inclusive culture where team members are inspired to celebrate your story, you need to look for ways to inspire growth and participation. There needs to be a dedicated effort to educate your internal team members on the impact they are having, while also illustrating their importance to the organization. The shared goal of the organization is to create a collaborative environment where you are growing these types of relationships inside and out.

YOUR PARTY IS READY TO START

We have often heard, "There is no I in Team," which relates to the idea that by "working together as one entity," we can achieve more. This is a fantastic principle, but we have graduated beyond this concept. Businesses don't need clones who memorize and recite mission statements on-demand. To create a great company and an even greater culture, individuality is essential.

Today, what businesses really need is for unified teams to stand up and commit to working TOGETHER as individuals who inject their own unique talents, personality, and ideas into the culture of the organization. Working TOGETHER as individuals means maintaining your own personality and perspective while choosing to join the celebration of the brand's story in partnership with other like-minded individuals. This allows you to be your best self, while also making a personal and deliberate choice to be a part of something bigger than yourself.

When you commit to working TOGETHER as an individual, you are making a conscious choice to overcome the barriers holding you back, to be strong, and to proudly join the celebration. If you hope to inspire this type of growth and change, that commitment needs to begin with you. You have to take ownership of your role in the story and choose to participate in a way that sets the organization up for success. This commitment is necessary to build the influence needed to inspire a brand celebration that will help your organization reach further, inspire change, and build real relationships.

The big I on the cover of this book represents the choice we can all make to graduate from an autonomous individual to an integrated Influencer.

Fears, doubts, and limiting beliefs will say that you are not enough to create this type of change, that your brand is not special enough to celebrate, or that people are not interested in hearing what you have to say. But don't let those voices distract you. If you want to take advantage of the opportunity to become an Influencer who inspires Influencers, you have to make a conscious, stated decision to reflect on these ideas and pursue something more.

Your story should be celebrated.

Believe that, and be inspired by the opportunity.

Today, everyone has the ability to be an Influencer. When a person joins in a celebration with commitment, passion, and purpose, they can multiply the effects of their actions and inspire a movement. The careful plans you have read in this book will help you achieve it. It takes commitment, but so does everything worth doing. It's time to get excited and go after it.

THE OPPORTUNITY

Before you march forward to begin your brand story celebration, you need to be armed with a few tools to ensure you are set to run your best race. The first advice is to keep two main takeaways front and center.

1. THIS TAKES WORK.

2. THE WORK IS REWARDING.

To execute the strategy and solutions in this book, you cannot step halfway into the process. You have to be all in if you want results.

William Arthur Ward once said, "Nothing limits achievement like small thinking; nothing expands possibilities like unleashed imagination." You can't unleash your imagination if you are handcuffed in doubt and disbelief. The first step is to produce an awareness of these obstacles. These are the barrier beliefs that create uncertainties, distract your mind, and impede your progress. For example:

> Nothing limits achievement like small thinking; nothing expands possibilities like unleashed imagination.

- If you fear that you are not strong enough to lead change in your organization, write it down.

- If you doubt that a team environment exists in your company, write it down.

- If your limiting belief is that social media and transparency are not important to your company because they are a waste of time, write it down.

Acknowledge these fears—don't just push them aside and expect them to go away. You have to consciously examine each one to see them for what they really are: weak, alluring excuses. It feels good to make an excuse because then we don't fail. We stop trying before we start. Recognizing excuses in this manner will empower you to take responsibility for their presence and deal with them out in the open.

Please take a moment to list the fears, doubts, and limiting beliefs that may impact your ability to be a leader.

ALLURING EXCUSES THAT HOLD ME BACK:

1. _____
2. _____
3. _____
4. _____
5. _____

Listing each of these alluring excuses creates an awareness that places you in a position of power. These restraints hold far less control when they are understood and acknowledged. In reviewing each sentence, make a plan to overcome any excuses and commit to taking action. Know that regardless of the outcome, progress will happen because you are stepping beyond your comfort zone, moving past the excuses, and committing yourself to giving your all. This is mindset management—choices made through awareness.

Are you going to allow these thoughts to fill your head and dictate your actions? Or are you going to stand up, recognize them, and walk past them to success?

You are choosing to graduate to a "Big I" Influencer, so after identifying these obstacles, use the power of "I" to overcome them. An "I" statement is a way to reclaim power, to assert our ability to influence, and to acknowledge our emotions. This process goes beyond feelings and turns them into commitments. Those are our "I statements": a declaration to be an Influencer who commits with passion, dedication, and of course, commitment.

Create an "I" statement for every excuse on your list. For example, you may rewrite the previous examples to include your new power perspective:

- I will powerfully inspire change by becoming a leader in my actions. I will not just talk about change. I will confidently back it up every day with my attitude and my visible commitment to the company.

- I wholeheartedly recognize that building our team mentality is a continual process. I will be a leader in developing this mentality by looking for every opportunity to assist my teammates, share experiences, and celebrate team participation.

- I acknowledge that the key to social media success is participation. I will commit to learning and finding ways in which I can contribute to the success of the program. I will also become a supporter of the program by getting others involved with it as well.

These sample statements take a weak, excuse-addled mindset and convert it into an "All In" power perspective. To do this, all you have to do is craft a statement to reposition your thoughts in a way that puts you in control over the emotion.

Each statement needs to serve as a commitment and promise to yourself to move past these obstacles, leaving you motivated and unrestrained.

MY ALL IN POWER PERSPECTIVES:

1. _____
2. _____
3. _____
4. _____
5. _____

Once freed from these emotions, your feelings will begin to change and you will be set to lead CDM. After making the switch, you don't need to look back. The baggage you left behind wasn't getting you anywhere, and you cannot be successful if you hold onto it. Brand celebrators are not led by negative emotions, but leaders who choose to direct their thoughts in order to lead a celebration, make a difference, and become an ultimate Influencer.

Leaders who follow this process are easy to recognize, and even easier to learn from. This book not only equips you with the ability to apply these principles in your own life, but also helps you develop an awareness of and appreciation for these traits in others. Look around and find influential brand celebrators that you can learn from every day. These are the Influencers who matter most. They generate influence by leading in a positive way, making an impact, and pushing themselves to go the extra mile.

As all the examples in this book have illustrated, stepping up, getting real, and leading with your brand can make all the difference in the world. You just need to be persistent. One of my favorite children's movies of all time is the Disney movie *Meet the Robinsons*. The animated movie is centered on a powerful quote from Walt Disney that represented his view of the Attitude, Drive, and Direction it takes to be successful:

Around here, however, we don't look backward for long. We keep moving forward, opening up new doors and doing new things ... and curiosity keeps leading us down new paths.

"Keep moving forward" was the central theme of the movie and words that the Robinson family used to guide their family culture. The film used this message to drive home the idea of failing forward when you make a mistake. That is the way CDM works: enthusiastic contribution, continual learning, positive growth, and forward progress. The story grows and progress happens through participation.

Remember, you aren't talking shit, you are being real and relatable. In real life, there are challenges and setbacks, and you deal with them by staying true to who you are. You never stop developing and adding to the story, you never stop defining yourself, and you never stop celebrating the assets of your brand.

This cycle of continual improvement is centered on the greatest opportunity that we all have: the freedom to choose our own path and define our own story. Regardless of what others are saying or doing, you have the ability to step up, celebrate your story, and become a Positive, Powerful, and Purposeful® Influencer. We all have this recourse. All you have to do is embrace the opportunity, believe in yourself, and keep moving forward.

Kelly Keenan is a leader in Brand Story development who formalized and trademarked a story development process for defining a brand's story in 2009. He is a brand strategist, agency owner, speaker, and leadership consultant. Over the past two decades, Kelly has helped hundreds of brands clarify their story to ignite their culture and sales.

He opened his first ad agency at the age of 24 and is the founder of Brand Story Experts, a full-service agency. BSE has specialized in the process of Culture Development Marketing powered by the 3-P Principle® since 2009. This process has been the starting point in every brand relationship at Brand Story Experts and the foundation for the success of the company.

In 2019, Kelly partnered in the development of The All In App. The All In App is an internal communications app, designed to facilitate the process of Culture Development Marketing by creating a cohesive system for brand education, training, and content development through the celebration of brand stories.

ACKNOWLEDGEMENTS

Every friend I've had over the last decade knows that finishing this book was not an easy task for me. It has taken many years of dedication and I could not have done it without the guidance and support of my family, friends, and colleagues.

First, I want to acknowledge my wife Samantha. You are not only beautiful inside and out, but you work harder than anyone I know. Your support and belief in me has not only helped me write this book, but together we have built a business and life that brings me joy every day.

To my three sons Kelly, Kyle, and Koby, you guys are fucking awesome. You don't read that kind of acknowledgement in business books too often, but I wanted to give you a shout out as unique as you are. God blessed me with three incredible sons and I am thankful for every minute that I get to be your father. Thank you for all the love, laughs, and support.

I got a break early in life and I was lucky enough to be born into a family of educators. Both of my parents and both of my brothers have their Ed.D., and I have benefitted greatly from their wisdom, guidance and support.

My father introduced me to leadership books, strategic planning, and culture building at an early age and I loved it. Those lessons planted the seeds that have allowed me to merge marketing and culture development into the perfect career for me. He also taught me to wake up early, to never talk shit, and to step up as a leader in life.

My mom is my heart. She gave me love, my artistic ability, and my appreciation of family. I know that I am blessed to have this type of guidance and I don't take it for granted.

I always say that I hit the lottery with my two brothers. Growing up in Ohio, many people suggested to me that it must have been tough to have brothers that were Valedictorians, All-State Football players, State Champion wrestlers, etc. But, the truth is that I never felt that pressure. Instead, I was honored to support their accomplishments and follow in their footsteps. They have been the ultimate influencers in my life by showing me the way academically, athletically, and professionally.

As for athletics, I have had many coaches and teammates impact my life. My high school wrestling coach John Craig will always be my favorite for a few reasons. First, because he is a coach who changes lives. His guidance has truly helped me to become a better athlete and, more importantly, a better person. Second, because he's a coach who taught me that talk is cheap. I'll never forget when I told him that my high school football coach repeatedly said that he could beat me in wrestling. Coach Craig invited him to back those words up in an exhibition before wrestling practice, and we all laughed at the result. Thank you for everything, Coach.

As the examples in this book detailed, I have also been fortunate to have learned from many people in my journey through the business world.

Early on, the Carapellotti family, Bob Nickerson, Mark Burch, Peggy Richmond, Kenny and Penny Davis, Perry and Janet Wade, my main man Mike Oliver, Super Bowl Champion Al Jenkins, Faris Alameh, Ann Gross, the late but great Bob Klein, and so many more were strong partners who blessed me with their trust, confidence, patience, and participation.

I dedicated this book to the Brand Story Experts that I have had the pleasure of working alongside because without their hard work, belief, and support we couldn't make an impact in the success and happiness of our partners.

Our Brand Story Experts journey has been fueled with love, support, and guidance from so many great individuals.

One of our first clients at BSE was Jaime DiDomenico. Our partnership has been a great success, and his company has grown through Culture Development Marketing. However, what has been even more special is the treasured friendship I gained. Thank you for the example you set every day by illustrating how true leaders focus on helping others succeed by taking care of people. You are my ambassador of Quan.

Thank you to Trevor Gooby for believing in our process and participating with us fully from the start. You are an incredible friend, you saved me from being hit by a car in New York City, and you became BSE's first viral news story when you delivered a baby at a baseball stadium. Does it get any better?

Thank you to the Pittsburgh Pirates for a winning partnership since 2009. We've had tremendous success, won awards, and had a lot of fun celebrating your story. Thank you for the opportunity to partner with a baseball team that's been my favorite since I was a kid.

I also want to express appreciation to my incredible partners and friends like Andy Ryan, Peter and Cheyenne Levi, John and Ann Gennaro, Randy Wadle, Glen Blavet, Rachelle Madrigal, Jeff Pdoobnik, Matt Morse, Rich Bogda, Jeff Ballard, John and Jackie Pankraz, John and Cheryl Dietz, Tom Doll, Tom Wells, Eric Swanson, the Neerings family, the Hucks, Matt Tyner, Julie DiDomenico, and Randy Baldwin. Your influence has taught me a lot about business and life.

A special thank you to Ken Haines, Meghann McNally, Andy and Travis Piercefield, Art Ragsdale and the Wrench Group for your trust in our process. You are the world's best in your industry and your support means a lot.

Thank you to the founders of Service Titan, Ara Mahdessian and Vahe Kuzoyan. It has been been a pleasure watching you grow. We met with you in the CoolToday offices when you were just getting started, and your software has enabled us to do so much more with your clients. Thank you for your support of our efforts and our events. Your software is incredible and you have been tremendous partners.

Thank you for the support of the Nexstar Network. It is inspiring to see the impact you make on so many business owners and teams. You are a team of educators just like us and our relationship over the past decade has helped us learn and grow.

I want to thank iPEC CEO Joan Ryan and the iPEC Coaching community. Your program was the missing ingredient I needed to formalize the process of Culture Development Marketing. I am grateful for the education and inspiration. Thank you also for introducing me to my iPEC instructor and friend for life, Dr. Shelby Hill. Shelby's insight and innovative work in leadership development has made a valuable impression, while helping to shape many views relayed in this book.

I have also been blessed to work with and be influenced by some of the best in the publishing world. Thank you to Janet Goldstein and Elizabeth Marshall for getting me started on my journey with this book. Thank you to Pam Slim, Kelly Kingman, Jen Repo, and Emily Angell for your assistance and guidance. Thank you to Todd Sattersten for the help in Portland and for pushing me to look at this project through a different lens. Also, a big shout out goes to Chris Johnson, you are a great friend and you were a big help on the final EIAI manuscript. I appreciate your brilliant mind, contagious enthusiasm, and unique style. You did awesome work in helping to get the headings and final content in order.

Immense gratitude to my publisher Rohit Bhargava. You brought tremendous wisdom to this project and connected me with a team of all-stars. I am thankful to have Chhavi Arya Bhargava, Marnie McMahon, Herb Schaffner, Jesse Tevelow, Sam Sarkisian, and the rest of the expansive Ideapress connections on my team. Thank you for helping me reshape the content and pushing me to the finish line.

Finally, I wanted to thank Dr. Dierdre Madden. Dr. Madden was the head of the Communications Department at Baldwin Wallace University when I attended. She taught several classes that I took over the first few years of attending BW. At the end of my third year, Dr. Madden learned that I had decided to switch my major, she called me and asked for a meeting.

Dr. Madden told me that she felt that I was very gifted in marketing and communications. She said she was surprised that I would change majors. I told her my family's success and experience made education seem like a more certain path. She then told me a story about her son. She explained that she had pushed him to take a safer path in life, but he chose the path he loved. She was a bit teary eyed as she reflected on how his success and happiness had taught her the power of doing what you love.

I left Dr. Madden's office, cancelled the switch to education and stayed the course. I graduated a year later in 1994, and since that time I have worked exclusively in the field of marketing/communications and I have loved every minute of it.

Dr. Madden celebrated a story about her son, that story inspired and influenced her, and she relayed that message to me—and that story changed my life. Dr. Madden passed away ten years after our meeting, and I never had a chance to tell her how much that meeting meant to me. However, every time I tell that story, the lesson she taught me lives on. She showed me that when you share inspiration that is authentic and real, Everyone can be an Influencer.

INDEX